Extreme NXT

Extending the LEGO MINDSTORMS NXT to the Next Level

▪ ▪ ▪

Michael Gasperi and
Philippe "Philo" Hurbain
with Isabelle Hurbain

Apress®

Extreme NXT: Extending the LEGO MINDSTORMS NXT to the Next Level

Copyright © 2007 by Michael Gasperi, Philippe Hurbain, Isabelle Hurbain

ISBN-13 (pbk): 978-1-59059-818-4

ISBN-10 (pbk): 1-59059-818-0

Printed and bound in the United States of America 9 8 7 6 5 4 3 2 1

Lead Editor: Jim Sumser
Technical Reviewer: Claude Baumann
Editorial Board: Steve Anglin, Ewan Buckingham, Gary Cornell, Jason Gilmore, Jonathan Gennick, Jonathan Hassell, James Huddleston, Chris Mills, Matthew Moodie, Dominic Shakeshaft, Jim Sumser, Keir Thomas, Matt Wade
Project Manager: Richard Dal Porto
Copy Edit Manager: Nicole Flores
Copy Editor: Susannah Davidson Pfalzer
Assistant Production Director: Kari Brooks-Copony
Production Editor: Ellie Fountain
Compositor: Kinetic Publishing Services, LLC
Proofreader: Nancy Riddiough
Indexer: Carol Burbo
Artist: Kinetic Publishing Services, LLC
Cover Designer: Kurt Krames
Manufacturing Director: Tom Debolski

Distributed to the book trade worldwide by Springer-Verlag New York, Inc., 233 Spring Street, 6th Floor, New York, NY 10013. Phone 1-800-SPRINGER, fax 201-348-4505, e-mail orders-ny@springer-sbm.com, or visit http://www.springeronline.com.

For information on translations, please contact Apress directly at 2560 Ninth Street, Suite 219, Berkeley, CA 94710. Phone 510-549-5930, fax 510-549-5939, e-mail info@apress.com, or visit http://www.apress.com.

The source code for this book is available to readers at http://www.apress.com in the Source Code/ Download section.

This book is dedicated to my dear wife, Jayne. Thanks for putting up with the mess I made on your desk. Love, Mike

I dedicate this book to my wife, Annie. She puts up with the pervasive invasion of LEGO and electronics parts everywhere, as well as with LEGO models "decorating" most of the shelves of our home. Thanks and love, Philo

To my fiancé, Pierre Palatin, who probably wished I went to bed earlier on many nights. I love you! Isa.

Contents at a Glance

Contents

Foreword

I am convinced that the developers of the LEGO RCX could neither have imagined the extraordinary success of their product, nor were they able to predict that the Programmable Brick would constitute a worldwide community of adult fans collaborating with—and to some extent, competing with—one another in miscellaneous domains, such as the creation of highly sophisticated LEGO robots or the design of astute sensors and actuators.

For almost a decade, this community has established itself and constantly grown. But during the last months it has gained strong impetus with the appearance of the LEGO NXT. Many members of the community are known to be excellent MINDSTORMERS, but only a handful of people have acquired the overall accepted—although unofficial—status of a *Master MINDSTORMER*.

The authors of this book are approved masters!

Michael Gasperi is one of the pioneers of extending the RCX functionality. Known as "Mr. Sensor," he initiated the development of compatible sensors. He also started a well-visited website, sharing details of his projects with RIS fans and setting up a collection of chosen links to other people's sensor pages that he was able to grab on the Internet. Meanwhile, Gasperi's "LEGO Mindstorms Sensor Input Page" has become the reference *par excellence* concerning the creation of homebrew sensors for any LEGO robotics amateur. With his experience and his ability to explain things clearly, Michael also participated as the coauthor of one of the best MINDSTORMS books: *Extreme MINDSTORMS: An Advanced Guide to LEGO MINDSTORMS* (Apress, 2000). His famous RCX input multiplexer has been published in the US electronics journal *Nuts and Volts*. These are the ideal prerequisites for continuing his work through this new book that is dedicated to the LEGO NXT. However, Mike felt that he would need the help of another MINDSTORMS geek.

Philippe "Philo" Hurbain is in fact the absolute opposite of a "geek." He is an enthusiast, for sure, and certainly one of the best LEGO experts, but he also is an active member of the MINDSTORMS community, lending a helping hand to anyone who is in trouble with his or her robot project. Philippe is a gifted photographer and has a particular sense of precision. Combining all his areas of expertise, Philo has created the neatest MINDSTORMS website, and has a long list of the most remarkable accomplishments. He has won a lot of prizes in LEGO extreme building contests; for example, with "Pimousse": a heavy-weight–lifting robot that is able to lift 44kg (97 pounds)! Philippe says about himself that his best programming tool is the soldering iron. He certainly is too modest here, because besides his extraordinary electronics skills, he also is an excellent MINDSTORMS programmer.

Philippe's daughter Isabelle always emphasizes that it is *her* Robotics Invention Set that her father is talking about. She has all my sympathy, because I remember the many times my own son asked me if he could play with the RCX, and I had to reply, "Wait a bit, I am currently working on a new project!" Definitely, two real MINDSTORMERS cannot share the same kit. Hopefully, the ownership of Hurbain's NXTs has been clarified. Anyway, Isabelle's influence on her father's projects cannot be denied, even if she works more discreetly in the background.

This book is the absolute *must* for any advanced LEGO robotics enthusiast who intends to become a master MINDSTORMER using the NXT. Compared to the RCX—already an outstanding device—the NXT sets the standard for the next generation of robot kits. By analogy, *Extreme NXT* represents the advanced part of the MINDSTORMS library and should not be missing on the specialist's bookshelf. Being lucky to have seen the book before printing, I was deeply impressed by the creativity and ingenuity of all of the chapters. First of all, the NXT MINDSTORMS kit is presented in a form that's typical for both Mike and Philo: all the sensors are taken apart so that the reader gets an insight into their interior and participates in reverse engineering. Remember that in the beginning of MINDSTORMS, it was a real surprise for LEGO to see adult freaks hacking its products, sharing their discoveries in open source projects, and thus becoming the real motor of the RCX's enormous success. That's certainly why LEGO voted for a new business strategy of sharing most of the NXT internals with the community, and even selecting 100 members of the community to be part of the MINDSTORMS Developer Program (MDP).

This book starts where its predecessors ended. The authors come right to the point with their central message: "Explore your NXT, play with it, and participate in unexpected experiments!" During the course of the book, you'll *learn by playing with problems*—one of Seymour Papert's constructivist postulates. You're asked to make your own NXT connector . . . and learn about how NXT talks to its sensors and motors; measure the salinity of water . . . and discover electric resistance; observe melting ice . . . and investigate the secrets of electronic temperature measurements; play music with Léon Theremin's organ . . . and understand the functioning of Light Dependent Resistors.

Like their Broom Balancer, the authors maintain the equilibrium of being explicit enough without ever getting lost in details. The practical, well-illustrated descriptions capture your attention with a note of humor. While explaining powered sensors, they introduce a Hall Effect Sensor and demonstrate its function with an NXT Robot Mouse seeking magnetic "cheese." The NXT edition of Mike's good old differential Light Sensor is converted into a sundial.

Later in the book, you're introduced to the secrets of the solderless breadboard and the PC board. To help you to overcome your hesitation to plunge into the complex world of integrated electronics, the book presents a most exciting experiment: an electronic whistler using a common light bulb filament! In another workbench project, a medical syringe and a pressure sensor serve to verify Boyle's Law. But even with these higher-ceiling projects, the authors stick to their rule of keeping things comprehensive and clear while using the NXT unexpectedly.

The authors investigate NXT output functionality through Button Pushers, Knob Twisters, Switch Flippers—names that reveal the authors' love for playing. In parallel, you learn how to change mechanical rotation into translation. You discover that you can use lamps, LEDs, Muscle Wires, electromagnets, and solenoids; finally, you build your own kinetic sculpture and a panoramic photographer robot. The I²C bus is explained on the basis of an absolutely amazing Magic Wall project, a reincarnation of the Simon game, a second edition of Philo's Color Sensor that's incorporated into a colored-brick–sorting robot, and an NXT version of the world's first video game, Pong. The NXT data-logging features are explored through measuring a hand warmer's temperature; Bluetooth is used with a remotely guided robot photographer.

Extreme NXT is a goldmine! Reading this book—and even more, working with it—will certainly produce new MINDSTORMS masters. By the way, the torch is passed to the NXT generation.

Claude Baumann
January 10, 2007

About the Authors

 **MICHAEL GASPERI** When I was growing up in the 1960s and '70s it made sense to build things, such as a computer, from component parts. In fact, you could build all kinds of electronic products, including television sets, this way. Not only does this not make any economic sense now, it is also physically impossible to deal with the tiny electronic components. Back then, magazines such as *Popular Electronics* provided all kinds of projects for the electronic hobbyist to experiment with. One of the regular columns was written by Forrest Mims III, and I eagerly anticipated reading his latest monthly installment. I always thought, "What a cool job this guy has; someday I'm going to do something like that."

I went to Purdue University, got an engineering degree, and ended up doing industrial research at Rockwell Automation. However, a part of me still yearned for the dream job of cooking up interesting projects and telling people how to do them. Back in 1998 LEGO introduced the MINDSTORMS Robotic Invention System. I naively bought a kit for my daughter Audrey, but quickly got swept up in the network of adult hackers trying to unlock the product's real potential. Through a simple personal web page I started publishing how the LEGO sensors worked and how to build new ones. This led to being invited to appear at MIT's MindFest and eventually to coauthoring a book on the subject, *Extreme MINDSTORMS: An Advanced Guide to LEGO MINDSTORMS* (Apress, 2000). Now that LEGO has introduced the next generation of MINDSTORMS, I felt compelled to experiment and write again.

 **PHILIPPE "PHILO" HURBAIN** Like Mike, I grew up in a time when electronics hobbies were widespread, and finding components and magazines was easy then. I built lots of gadgets, and also measurement instruments. One of my biggest projects was also my first robot: a wall-avoiding car that was wire programmable, using components unsoldered from old IBM mainframe boards.

While studying engineering at École Centrale de Paris, I assembled my first "computer" in a time when 16K was considered a huge amount of memory. After I got my degree, I worked a few years for a French computer startup, then I created a small design house with three fellow students where I designed communication boards (ISDN then ADSL).

About 20 yeas ago I discovered LEGO Technic. I used them to build an equivalent of my old wall-avoiding car. That was my first LEGO "bot." However, there were no standard LEGO parts for what I needed and I didn't have time to learn how to build complicated LEGO models, so I tired of it. But then the Robotics Invention System 1.5 reached France, and it looked wonderful, so I bought one for my daughter. Of course I ended up playing with the set a lot more than she did. I was hooked!

I started describing my constructions and RCX electronics add-ons in a website, which got me some recognition from fellow builders, and even from LEGO, who chose me as one of 100 beta testers for its new NXT robotics set. In this book I'll share some ideas, tips, and tricks learned during this exciting period.

 ▪**ISABELLE HURBAIN** As Philo's daughter, I've grown up in a house where there was always something new: computers, Penrose tilings, fractals, and of course LEGO. I was much more a LEGO-liking than a doll-liking kind of girl! I fondly remember the solder odor that was quite frequent at home.

The familial legend says that I was playing on the Apple II's pinball simulation when I was 1½ years old, and winning; I think I literally got into computers before speaking. Unfortunately (and to Philo's greater despair), I was quite a bad student in physics and electronics. Not that I wasn't trying—it just didn't catch on with my brain. Philo has often helped me when my studies required me to do anything involving a transistor!

My math was much better though, and this allowed me to enter the École des Mines de Nantes, a French engineering school. Against popular wisdom, I choose my major in automatic control and industrial computing and not in pure CS—I thought it would be more interesting that way. This helped me while writing this book.

After my engineering degree, I began a PhD thesis (still not finished at the time of writing) in CS, and in parallel, got some experience in technical translation and writing. This is why, when Philo asked me if I could help putting his ideas on paper for this book, I was more than happy to help him. I hope I did a good job translating his work into words.

About the Technical Reviewer

Since 1999, **CLAUDE BAUMANN** has taught advanced LEGO MINDSTORMS robotics in after-school classes and maintains the related widely known website `http://www.convict.lu/Jeunes/RoboticsIntro.htm`. He participated in beta testing of the ROBOLAB software that originated from Tufts University. He also has been in charge—in collaboration with Professor Chris Rogers—of the creation of ULTIMATE ROBOLAB, a cross-compiler environment that allows graphical programming of RCX firmware, and of a unique RCX self-replicating program (also called a "virus"). Claude has been the assessor of various high school robot projects (among which is the famous LEGO humanoid robot GASTON) and is the author and coauthor of several related articles and conference presentations. In 2004 and 2005, he was guest speaker at the Annual ROBOLAB Conference in Austin, Texas. He's married and has three children, is the director of a boarding institution in Luxembourg, and is the radio amateur LX1BW.

Acknowledgments

This book wouldn't have happened without my friend Dave Baum. Back in 2000 Dave got me started as a writer by convincing me to coauthor with him on the *Extreme MINDSTORMS* book. When LEGO announced it was introducing a new generation of MINDSTORMS, it made sense to write a similar book. Fortunately, Dave received one of the early-release NXT kits, and he generously loaned it to me so I could jump start the book development process. Thanks again, Dave.

Michael Gasperi

The true father of this book is Mike. He had to convince me that we should coauthor a book on our common passion: hacking the new NXT. So, thanks a lot, Mike, for leading me in this adventure! I'd also like to thank LEGO for creating this outstanding product, and for choosing me as a beta tester.

Philippe Hurbain

I'd like to thank my father, Philippe Hurbain, without whom I wouldn't have had the opportunity to work on this book, and who put me back on the "LEGO track." I'd also like to thank Mike Gasperi, who really was the one who held this book and our small team together. And a final thank you to my whole family and all my friends for being so supportive of all my activities.

Isabelle Hurbain

Introduction

Before you get overly involved in extending the NXT, you need to understand the history of the MINDSTORMS concept and the hardware and software that LEGO makes for it. In Chapter 2 we discuss the NXT and the RCX-compatible sensors and motors. Let's void the warranty by taking them apart and seeing what's inside. We'll also provide a brief introduction to NXT-G and two alternative languages: Next Byte Codes (NBC) and RobotC. Chapter 3 covers the ins and outs of the NXT and how to connect to it.

The simplest types of sensors to homebrew are generically referred to as *passive sensors*. Contact, resistive, potentiometer, and voltage sensors usually only require a single electronic part, but despite their apparent simplicity, they can be used to create some interesting projects. Chapters 4, 5, 6, and 7 contain plans for projects such as a surfboard game, an antenna sensor, an ohmmeter, temperature and humidity sensors, a theremin musical instrument, a model of Braitenberg's vehicle, a digital protractor, two joysticks, and a battery tester.

The 4.3V powered sensors aren't a lot more complicated than the passive ones, but you can build even more interesting projects with them. In Chapter 8 we'll look at the Hall Effect, infrared rangefinder, and differential Light Sensors. With them you can build a robot mouse that looks for magnetic cheese, a vehicle that follows walls, and a digital sundial.

Things get a little more complicated when we look at two-wire powered sensors in Chapter 9. They have a higher power supply voltage, and that allows you to use integrated circuit operational amplifiers to measure very small voltages. The projects include a half volt voltmeter, hot wire anemometer, and calibrated pressure sensor.

HiTechnic, mindsensors.com, and Techno-stuff are aftermarket makers of accessories for the NXT. In Chapter 10 we'll look at some of their offerings and discuss how they're used. DCP Microdevelopments and Vernier sell equipment designed for laboratory use, and they also sell adapters that allow you to hook up a huge range of sensors to the NXT.

Not every extension to the NXT requires building new hardware. The NXT can control appliances by using its motor to push buttons, turn knobs, or flip switches on them. In Chapter 11 we'll show examples of operating a wireless remote control to make an NXT version of the Clapper, turning the knobs on an Etch A Sketch to make an Etch-A-NXT, and flipping a pneumatic switch to open and close a simple robotic gripper.

By Chapter 12 you'll be ready to go beyond the NXT motor. Some new outputs are easy, such as lamps, LEDs, Muscle Wires, and electromagnets. Others, such as relays and power amplifiers, allow you to connect the NXT to much bigger loads. The projects in the chapter include a decision maker, a kinetic sculpture, several motor controls, and ways to connect two loads to the same output.

The ultimate interface to the NXT is its I^2C bus. It allows the NXT to be connected to intelligent sensors and expanded to have practically unlimited inputs and outputs. In Chapter 13, we'll go into the details of building a benchmark I^2C port. From there you can build a magic wand display, a Simon game, a relay output, and a Color Sensor.

Chapter 14 is a collection of cool projects that involve combining the NXT with other things. You'll use spreadsheet programs, other NXTs, LEGO trains, and digital cameras to conduct a data logging experiment, remotely control a vehicle, automatically control a train station, take some panoramic photos, and play a game of Pong.

Constructing electronic projects like the ones in this book might be new to you. Appendix A will show you how to build an electronic circuit on a solderless breadboard and then how to move it to a printed circuit board to make it permanent. It even takes you through the basics of soldering. Appendix B has sources for components, website links, and other references where you can learn more. Appendix C has the full listings of the programs only partially shown in the chapters. The book website in the Source Code/Download area of http://www.apress.com has the programs and CAD drawings of the projects for you to download.

CHAPTER 1

■■■

In the Beginning

LEGO launched the MINDSTORMS NXT in the fall of 2006, but our story really begins eight years earlier in the fall of 1998, when LEGO introduced the first MINDSTORMS kit: The Robotics Invention System (RIS) with the Robotic Control Explorer (RCX) programmable brick (see Figure 1-1). It represented the evolution of five decades of modular construction techniques from LEGO, with years of computer-based education methods from the Massachusetts Institute of Technology (MIT).

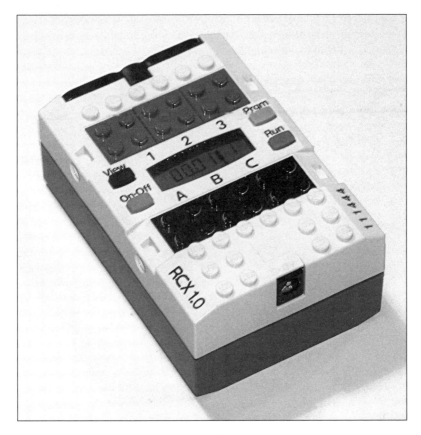

Figure 1-1. *The Robotic Command Explorer (RCX) circa 1998*

LEGO had been producing construction toys since the late 1940s, starting with the familiar interlocking building blocks and ending with today's highly technical pieces, which include beams, motors, gears, and pneumatics. Although the style of building has changed, the new pieces are designed to be backward compatible and interoperable with the old. This compatibility feature, and the huge inventory of parts, are some of the reasons why LEGO is such an attractive choice for construction.

MIT had been investigating the use of computers in education from the late 1970s. The name MINDSTORMS was actually taken from a book title by MIT computer scientist Seymour Papert. The work involved the concept of not just using computers to deliver tests and evaluate children, but also for children to use computers themselves for problem solving and invention. Originally the computers were so large they had to be external to the inventions, but as technology allowed, they became a part of the creation itself through a myriad of prototype programmable bricks.

The RCX and the Robotics Invention System

The RIS was revolutionary because, for the first time, people could easily share complex inventions. Everyone could build exactly the same invention without traditional skills such as carpentry, metal working, electronics, and programming. It was also a boon for educational institutions that needed a durable and reusable platform for engineering lab projects. Figure 1-2 shows the more than 700 parts included with the RIS.

Figure 1-2. *The original Robotics Invention System (RIS), circa 1998*
Photo courtesy of LEGO

CHAPTER 1 ■ IN THE BEGINNING

The RCX had an eight-bit computer, three inputs, three outputs, infrared communications, a speaker, and a four-digit LCD display. It was programmed on a personal computer with a simple graphical language that vaguely resembled the stacking building blocks. Due to serious oversimplification, the language was practically useless for anything but the most primitive designs. People immediately started to reverse engineer, or hack, the product. The shortcomings of the minimal hardware also put pressure on the effort.

Back in 1998, the Internet was still relatively new. Most people accessed it through slow dial-up connections, and the main collaboration tools were newsgroups and e-mail lists. People around the world started feverishly exploring the RCX, discovering and then reporting to everyone on the Internet what they had found. Despite limited communications, the effort pioneered by Kekoa Proudfoot and Russell Nelson led Dave Baum, Ralph Hempel, and Markus Noga to introduce alternative languages, and Michael Gasperi to publish designs for homebrew sensors within months. These were exciting times.

This all seems to have come as a surprise to the people at LEGO, who expected children simply to accept the product for what it was, and didn't expect adults to dissect it. However, they eventually embraced the effort by publishing Software Development Kits (SDKs) and other documentation to make the RCX a more open platform. They were even present when MIT hosted a gathering of the early hackers in 1999 called Mindfest.

Following the RCX, LEGO introduced a more limited programmable brick called the Scout in the Robotics Discovery System (RDS). It was targeted for a younger audience than the RIS, who had less interest in programming. Because its operating system was in unchangeable read-only memory (ROM), it was doomed to be ignored by the hackers. Even more ignored were the even more limited Micro Scout and the Droid Developer Kit, which wasn't much more than a programmable motor. Although Vision Command offered some sophisticated image processing capability, it was really a Windows application and only used the RCX as a kind of output device.

It all felt as if LEGO was going in the wrong direction. Instead of constantly improving, the new MINDSTORMS products were getting weaker and more limited. In a world where electronics become obsolete in months, the RCX stood for eight years virtually unchanged. Embraced by the education community, it became a classroom fixture, serving as a platform for teaching programming and a wide range of engineering topics.

The MINDSTORMS NXT

The MINDSTORMS NXT (see Figure 1-3) is an enhancement in every aspect to the original RIS. In particular, the NXT programmable brick shown in Figure 1-4 has a 32-bit microprocessor, four inputs, three outputs, Bluetooth communications, a speaker, and a 100×64 LCD display. Also, the NXT includes three powerful motors with built-in rotation sensors. The graphical programming language, NXT-G, is simple but complete enough to be usable.

Figure 1-3. *MINDSTORMS NXT*

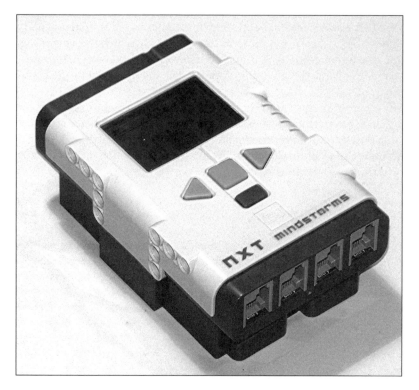

Figure 1-4. *The NXT programmable brick*

LEGO didn't just improve on the product; it went about improving the product launch as well. One hundred NXT kits were distributed months ahead of the major launch to a hand-selected group through the MINDSTORMS Developer Program (MDP) to work out any remaining issues. LEGO even provided detailed product documentation and SDKs well in advance. Aftermarket sensor manufacturers and software developers were able to have products available immediately, as opposed to months later for the RIS.

Sadly, there was only a small network of NXT hackers, but that doesn't take away from what the NXT can do. Its programming language is quite usable; there's an extra input, three sophisticated motors, and more types of sensors; and it is well-documented. Often hackers felt disappointed that they still couldn't build what they wanted even after they went to lengths to reverse engineer the RCX. Not that there aren't ways to go beyond what comes in the MINDSTORMS NXT box—LEGO couldn't possibly provide every sensor or actuator that could be used for building inventions, and that's where this book fits in.

■ ■ ■

CHAPTER 2

In the Box

Before you jump into building your own sensors and actuators, it's important to understand the ones that came in the box, and a few that didn't. It's also important to understand the programming languages available to the NXT and their strengths and weakness.

The Sensors

Sensors provide feedback to a system telling it where it is or how it's doing. The NXT has several types of sensors designed specifically for it, and backward compatibility to the old RCX sensors. All the sensors are well documented by LEGO, but we'll provide additional characteristics and show the internal construction of the sensors.

NXT Sensors

The NXT comes with five types of sensors: Touch, Light, Sound, Ultrasonic, and Rotation. The NXT Rotation Sensor is conveniently built into its motor so shaft position and speed are always available to NXT programs.

Touch

The NXT Touch Sensor is shown in Figure 2-1. A nice feature of the Touch Sensor is its cross hole that allows you to connect the sensor operator directly to other assemblies. Internally the Touch Sensor is a printed circuit board (PCB) mounted push button and a connector, as seen in Figure 2-2. There's also a resistor in series with the switch so it won't create a dead short if it's accidentally connected to an output port.

Figure 2-1. *NXT Touch Sensor*

Figure 2-2. *Touch Sensor breakdown*

Light

The NXT Light Sensor includes a Light Emitting Diode (LED) light source that can be turned on and off from software (see Figures 2-3 and 2-4). This allows you to measure either the reflected LED light shining back from an object or the ambient light falling on the sensor. In Figure 2-3 you can see the LED, phototransistor, and connector mounted on the top of the PCB. All the small surface-mounted electronics are on the bottom of the board.

Figure 2-3. *NXT Light Sensor*

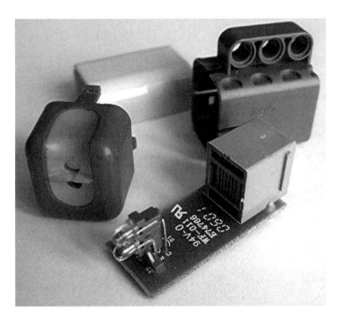

Figure 2-4. *Light Sensor breakdown*

The phototransistor in the Light Sensor is far more sensitive to the infrared colors of light than the relatively narrow visible spectrum we see. This can be confusing, because it sees hot light sources such as incandescent light bulbs as being much brighter than we do. Figure 2-5 shows how the transistor's spectral response overlaps the human eye.

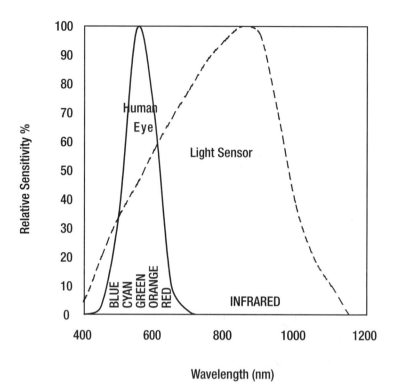

Figure 2-5. *Light Sensor spectral response*

We'll discuss light sensitivity in more detail in Chapter 5 when we make our own Light Sensors. Looking ahead, Table 5-1 has the average light intensity of various locations. Figure 2-6 shows the sensitivity of the NXT sensor over a wide range of light intensities, which is usually measured in units of lux (lx).

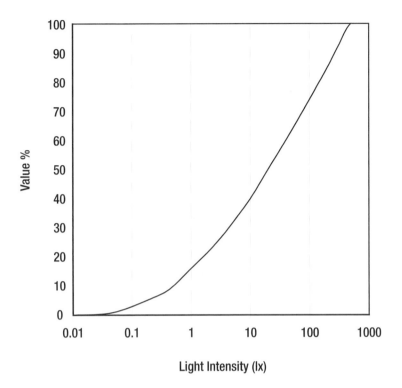

Figure 2-6. *Light Sensor sensitivity*

Sound

Surprisingly, LEGO didn't provide the RCX with a Sound Sensor. Because it's such a natural type of input, the Sound Sensor was one of the first sensors to be widely homebrewed. The NXT Sound Sensor (see Figure 2-7) is constructed much like the Light Sensor. In Figure 2-8 you can see the microphone mounted in plastic foam, a capacitor, and the connector on the top of the PCB with the rest of the electronics mounted on the bottom.

Figure 2-7. *NXT Sound Sensor*

Figure 2-8. *Sound Sensor breakdown*

Sound volume or sound pressure level (SPL) is measured in units called decibels (dB). Rather than an absolute measurement such as lux, decibels measure how much a sound level is relatively louder or softer than another sound. In this case, 0dB is the faintest sound that an average person can hear. Table 2-1 lists some typical dB values, and Figure 2-9 shows the NXT Sound Sensor sensitivity.

Table 2-1. *Sound Pressure Levels*

SPL dB	Source
90	Loud noises
80	Shouting
70	Talking
60	Office/talking at a distance
50	Quiet living room

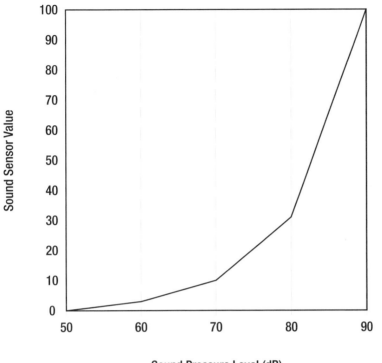

Figure 2-9. *Sound level value versus sound pressure level*

Looking back at Figure 2-5, you can see that human vision has peak sensitivity to green light and drops off to zero toward both blue and red. Human sound sensitivity also has a peak. It's around 3kHz, and drops off to zero toward both 20Hz and 20kHz. The Sound Sensor can be put into a dBA mode where the sound reading more closely matches that of the human ear.

Ultrasonic

Avoiding objects is one of the first objectives for a robot. Most of the time it's better not to even touch objects, and that's where the NXT Ultrasonic Sensor comes in (see Figure 2-10). The guts of the sensor are shown in Figure 2-11. The two cylindrical objects connected with wires to the PCB are the ultrasonic speaker and microphone.

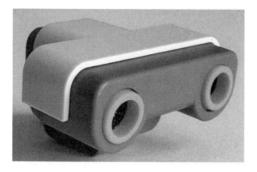

Figure 2-10. *NXT Ultrasonic Sensor*

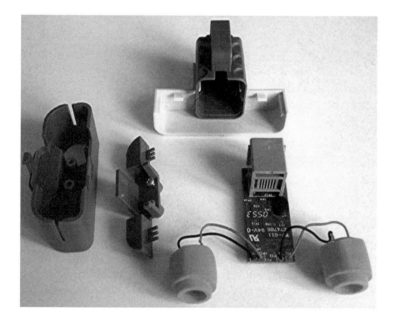

Figure 2-11. *Ultrasonic Sensor breakdown*

It's such a complex sensor that it needs its own microprocessor. Because of this added intelligence, it reports distance in absolute units rather than on some relative scale like the Light and Sound Sensors. The sensor works just like sonar by sending out a short burst of ultrasonic sound at 40kHz. It then measures the time it takes for the sound to travel out to an object, reflect, and travel back. If there's only one large object, such as a flat wall, in front of the sensor, the measurement is quite good. However, if the scene becomes complicated, such as with many small objects, it isn't as reliable.

RCX Sensors

The Robotics Invention System included two Touch Sensors and one Light Sensor. There was also a Temperature Sensor that could be ordered separately. The Rotation Sensor had to be ordered separately too, and this was a serious drawback because Rotation Sensors are critical to building complex projects. It also consumed one of the three RCX input ports, unlike the NXT built-in Rotation Sensor. All the RCX sensors require the conversion cable (LEGO #8528) to connect them to the NXT.

Touch

The RCX Touch Sensor in Figure 2-12 uses the same conductive rubber technology found in the buttons of calculators and remote controls (see Figure 12-13). The operator lacks a way to connect directly to it, and it also doesn't move back and forth very far, which makes constructing reliable bumpers difficult.

Figure 2-12. *RCX Touch Sensor*

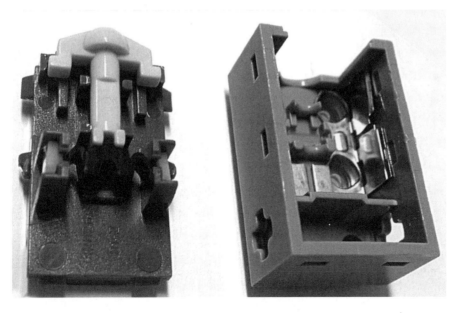

Figure 2-13. *Touch Sensor breakdown*

Light

The RCX Light Sensor also contains an LED light source, but it's always turned on (see Figure 2-14). The sensor is built into a brick, and you can see its internal construction in Figure 2-15. It uses a phototransistor like the NXT Light Sensor, and has similar infrared spectral sensitivity. The light sensitivity is also comparable to the NXT, but partly due to physical placement of the always-on LED and the phototransistor, the RCX Light Sensor has notoriously poor sensitivity to low light. It seldom has a light reading below ten.

Figure 2-14. *RCX Light Sensor*

Figure 2-15. *Light Sensor breakdown*

Rotation

The RCX Rotation Sensor resolves 16 locations per rotation or 22.5 degrees (see Figure 2-16). Internally, it detects the vanes on a rotating shaft with two opto-interrupters. An opto-interrupter is a phototransistor and an LED that are pointed at each other with a small gap in between. The RCX or NXT watches the states of the two interrupters to determine which direction the sensor is rotating, and increments or decrements a counter accordingly. Unfortunately, at low speed, the sensor has some problems with losing counts. You can see the vanes and the electronics on the PCB in Figure 2-17.

Figure 2-16. *RCX Rotation Sensor*

Figure 2-17. *Rotation Sensor breakdown*

The RCX Rotation Sensor has one big advantage over the NXT. Because it hasn't been combined with an elaborate gear train and electric motor, the RCX Rotation Sensor rotates almost without friction. If you want to measure the rotation of something like a hamster wheel, you need the RCX Rotation Sensor.

Temperature

The RCX Temperature Sensor looks like a brick with a metal tube sticking out of it (see Figure 2-18). The temperature transducer is located inside this metal tube. We'll discuss the sensor in great detail in Chapter 5 when you make your own Temperature Sensor.

Figure 2-18. *RCX Temperature Sensor*

The Motors

Direct Current (DC) motors always rotate too quickly to be connected directly to wheels and other loads. Some sort of gear train is necessary to lower the speed, which conveniently increases the torque. Both the NXT and RCX motors have built-in gear reduction. You might run across several other LEGO motors, but these two are the only ones that can be ordered as accessories for the NXT.

NXT Motor

The NXT motor is an impressive combination of gear reduction and feedback sensing (see Figure 2-19). The gear reduction alone involves eight different gears, and because the Rotation Sensor is way back by the motor end, it has one degree of revolution on the output shaft. You can see the gears and Rotation Sensor in the breakdown shown in Figure 2-20. The NXT Rotation Sensor works on the same principle as the RCX Rotation Sensor, only on a smaller scale, as seen in the close-up photo in Figure 2-21.

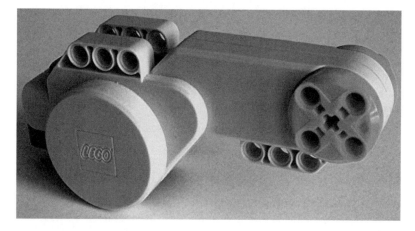

Figure 2-19. *NXT motor*

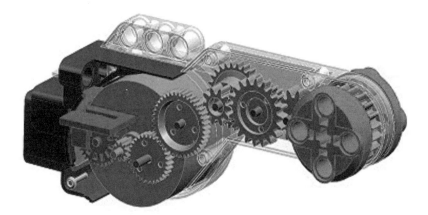

Figure 2-20. *Motor breakdown*

Figure 2-21. *Close-up of Rotation Sensor*

RCX Motor

The RCX motor (see Figure 2-22) is internally geared down too, but not as much as the NXT motor. It might be appropriate where you need high speed but low torque, because the motor isn't as powerful as the NXT motor. The DC motor brushes are visible on the back of the motor in the breakout photograph in Figure 2-23. It requires the conversion cable (LEGO #8528) to connect it to the NXT. A unique feature of the old RCX-style connector is that, depending on the orientation of the mating connectors, you can reverse the motor direction without changing the software.

Figure 2-22. *RCX motor*

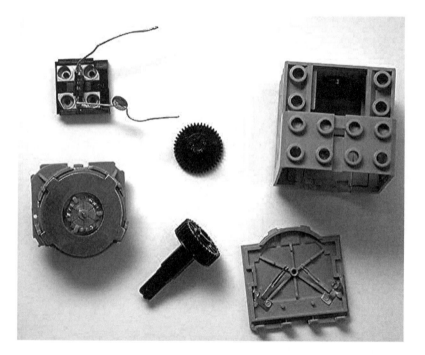

Figure 2-23. *Motor breakdown*

The Lamp

LEGO makes a little light in a 1×2 brick shown in Figure 2-24. You could potentially use it with the Light Sensor to make an opto-interrupter, or it can just be another type of indicator. Unfortunately, it isn't very bright, even with full power. It needs the conversion cable, but it can be conveniently plugged directly on the RCX end of the cable.

Figure 2-24. *The LEGO 9V lamp*

The Languages

This book is primarily about building hardware, but software is always involved too. The different languages available to the NXT are documented well enough without repeating it here. We expect that newer and better languages will come along for the NXT as time goes by.

NXT-G

NXT-G is the programming language that comes in the box. The development environment window looks like Figure 2-25. The language is highly graphical, consisting of blocks that perform operations such as input, output, computation, and execution flow. You can download the NXT-G program to the NXT and perform other maintenance functions from the same environment.

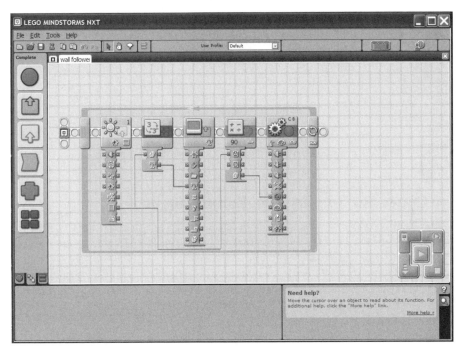

Figure 2-25. *NXT-G programming environment*

Data is passed from block to block on "data wires." For example, the first block in the program shown in Figure 2-26 is a Light Sensor. The light level as a percent number (0 to 100) is being passed to the Number to Text block and also to a Math block. You can minimize the blocks to show only the inputs and outputs that are being used by clicking the top of the data hub. Figure 2-27 shows the neater and more compact version of the same program. You can add comments, such as the number 90 on the Math block, to make it easier to read the program.

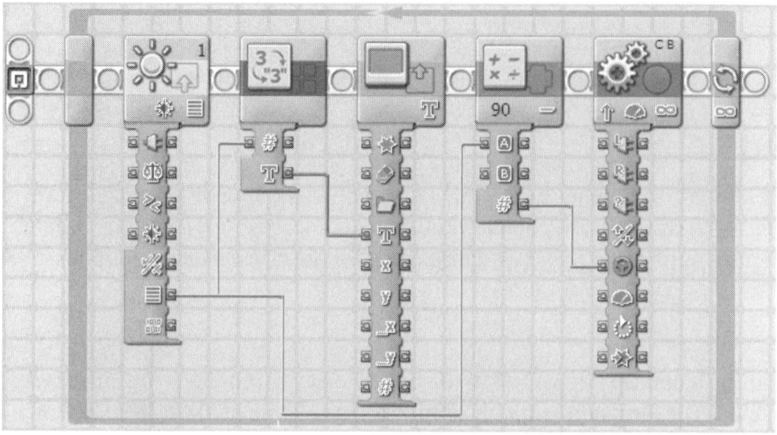

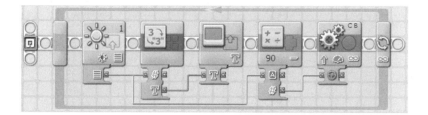

Figure 2-26. *NXT-G program with expanded blocks*

Figure 2-27. *NXT-G program with blocks minimized*

Next Byte Codes and the BricxCC Environment

Next Byte Codes (NBC) is on the other end of the programming spectrum from NXT-G. One NXT-G block might represent ten or more NBC lines of code. However, NBC gives you more complete control of the NXT, and allows you to generate code that NXT-G can't. BricxCC is a programming environment (see Figure 2-28) originally developed for the RCX and a language called Not Quite C (NQC). It has been upgraded to include the NXT and NBC. Although you can use NBC without a programming environment, BricxCC makes it much more enjoyable.

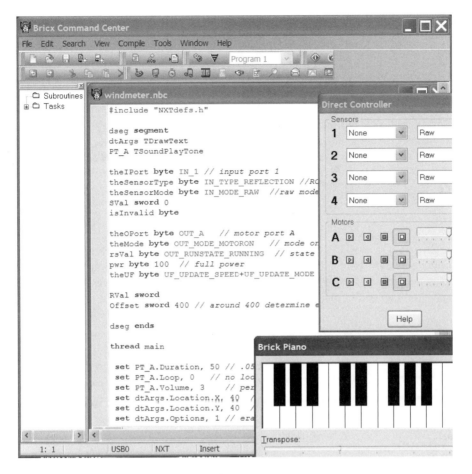

Figure 2-28. *BricxCC programming environment*

Listing 2-1 shows a simple NBC program that prints the words "Hello World" on the NXT display. No doubt NBC will evolve to make programming easier than this. The declarations part of the program isn't really doing anything, but it's overhead that needs to be included. It isn't till the part labeled main that the program actually starts by setting some values and then making the system call to DrawText to finally print the text.

Listing 2-1. *NBC Hello World Program*

```
#include "NXTDefs.h"

dseg segment
text TDrawText    //text is structure for DrawText
dseg ends

thread main
set text.Location.X, 1       //text will be at 1,1
set text.Location.Y, 1
```

```
set text.Options, 1        //option 1 clears screen
mov text.Text, 'Hello World' //the actual text to draw
syscall DrawText, text     //call to actually draw the text
Forever:
  jmp Forever              //loop forever
endt
```

This might all look a bit tedious to you, and it is for a program this simple. However, although NXT-G has variables, using them in a program can also be tedious. You need separate blocks to read and write variables, and just adding one to a variable uses three blocks. The good news is that NBC and BricxCC are both freeware, so you can try them with no risk. We'll look at some longer examples of NBC programs in Chapters 9 and 10.

RobotC

RobotC is somewhere between NXT-G and NBC in complexity. It has an integrated programming environment, as shown in Figure 2-29. Unlike NBC, it replaces the LEGO firmware in the NXT, and you'll have to purchase RobotC. Hopefully, that means you'll get better documentation and support than for something that's free.

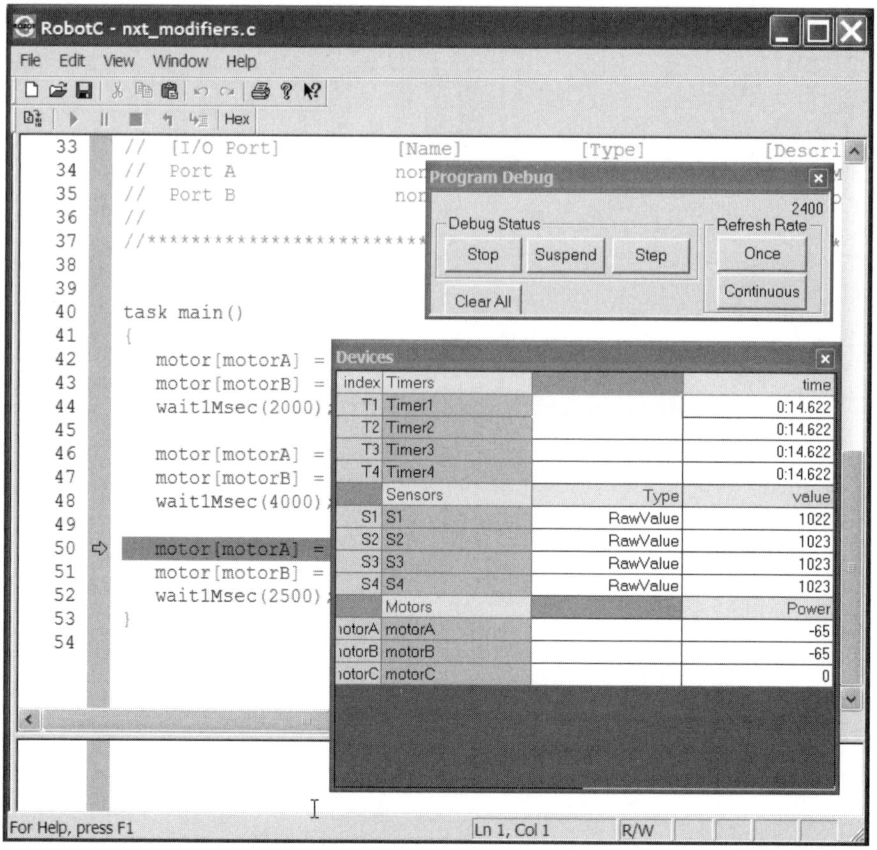

Figure 2-29. *RobotC programming environment*

Listing 2-2 shows a short example RobotC program. One curious part of RobotC is the programming wizard that pops up and configures the NXT input and output ports. It created the first line in the program that configures port 1 as a Touch Sensor. The rest of the program follows the C language style and should be fairly self explanatory.

Listing 2-2. *RobotC Touch Program*

```
const tSensors touch = (tSensors) S1;

task main()
{
      eraseDisplay();
      while (true)
      {
         if (SensorBoolean[touch])
         {
             nxtDisplayTextLine(5, "Pressed    ");
         }
         else
         nxtDisplayTextLine(5, "Not Pressed");
      }
}
```

CHAPTER 3

Connecting to the NXT

Before you can start homebrewing sensors and extending the outputs, you need to understand how to connect to the NXT. In this chapter, we'll describe the unusual connector used on the NXT and define the electrical signals found on the ports. We'll even show you some simple ways to build sensors and adapters.

NXT Ports

The four sensor input ports are on the bottom of the NXT, and they're numbered from 1 to 4. The three motor output ports are on the top of the NXT, and they're labeled A, B, and C. If you look through the clear plug on the end of an NXT cable, you can see the six pins and wires that make up the interface. The wires are color coded: white, black, red, green, yellow, and blue. The function of the wires depends on whether they're used on a sensor input or a motor output. Their function even depends on what type of sensor is connected.

Sensor Input Pinout and Signal Description

Table 3-1 sums up the colors and names of the pins for a sensor input port.

Table 3-1. *Colors and Names of the Input Pins*

Pin number	Color	Name
1	White	AN
2	Black	GND
3	Red	GND
4	Green	4.3V Power
5	Yellow	DIGI0
6	Blue	DIGI1

Pin 1—White—AN

You can use the first pin for two purposes: either as an analog input or as a 9V power supply used for compatibility with the old RCX sensors.

When you use the pin as an analog input, the signal is connected to a 10-bit analog-to-digital converter. The input signal can range from 0 to 5V, and is translated into a raw digital value between 0 and 1023. The value is sampled every 3 milliseconds. The pin is permanently connected to 5V through a 10KΩ pull-up resistor, and in the next few chapters you'll see how that simplifies many sensor designs.

You can also use the first pin as a 9V power supply. The voltage is actually that of the batteries. If you use NiMH batteries, you'll only be able to get about 7.2V from this output. You can use this power supply to power sensors that need higher voltages. For example, the RCX Light Sensor uses this power supply, and the NXT Ultrasonic Sensor also uses the supply to get more power for its transmitter.

For these sensors, the NXT powers the sensor for 3 milliseconds and reads the value for 0.1 milliseconds. The sensor needs a capacitor to store power during the read interval. Figure 3-1 shows the output voltage at different loads with new batteries. There is a current limit of approximately 14 mA per input port. If the current is greater than this value, the voltage rapidly drops.

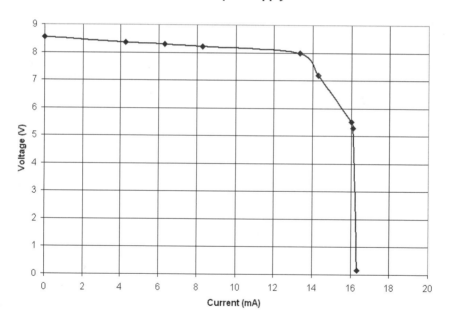

Figure 3-1. *Sensor 9V voltage versus current*

Pins 2 and 3—Black and Red—GND

The second and third pins are ground pins. These two pins are connected together in the NXT and in LEGO sensors. All signals are measured referring to these ground pins. Your sensor can use either pin, or both.

Pin 4—Green—4.3V Power

This is the main power supply for all NXT sensors. As opposed to the 9V power supply, this power supply has a total current limit of 180 mA for all seven input and output ports. Every port can use 25 mA on average, but it's also possible to consume more current on one port if another consumes less. For example, the currents for the NXT standard sensors and motor encoders are presented in Table 3-2.

Table 3-2. *Current Consumption of the NXT Sensors and Motors Encoders*

Device	Measured
Touch	0
Sound	1.7 mA
Light Sensor (light off)	2.6 to 3 mA (depends on light)
Light Sensor (light on)	16.3 mA
Ultrasonic Sensor	4 mA
Motor position encoders	9 to 12 mA (depends on encoder position)
All RCX sensors and motors (via cable adapter)	0

Figure 3-2 shows how the power supply voltage drops with increasing load. It approaches 5V with no load, and is only 4.3V with a fairly substantial load. This would not be a good power supply for integrated circuits with 5V logic, but newer technology digital-logic parts can be powered from it.

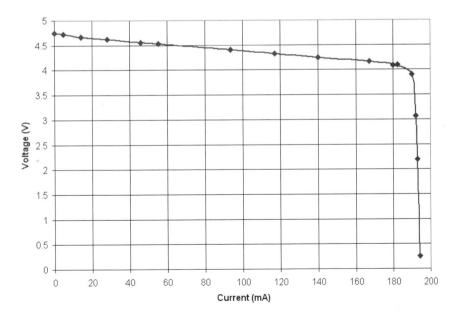

Figure 3-2. *Sensor 4.3V voltage versus current*

Pins 5 and 6—Yellow and Blue—DIGI0 and DIGI1

These pins are 3.3V digital signals and are directly connected to the NXT's microprocessor. They are primarily used for I²C communications, which we'll discuss in Chapter 13. When the pins are used as outputs, you need to be aware of the 3.3V limit. When they're used as input, the NXT has protection circuitry to prevent higher voltages from damaging anything. This circuit includes a 4.7kΩ resistor connected in series with the port. That way, even if the voltage of the sensor is too high, the corresponding current will be low, so that the electronics aren't damaged.

In addition to I²C communications, DIGI0 is used for the NXT Light Sensor to command the state of the light emitting diode: on (reflection mode) or off (ambient light). It's also used in the Sound Sensor to switch between the DB mode (raw sound level) and the DBA mode (filtered sound level to close it up from the sensibility of the human ear).

Motor Output Pinout

Table 3-3 sums up the colors and names of the pins for a motor output.

Table 3-3. *Colors and Names of the Output Pins*

Pin Number	Color	Name
1	White	M1
2	Black	M2
3	Red	GND
4	Green	4.3V POWER
5	Yellow	TACHO0
6	Blue	TACHO1

Pin 1 and 2—White and Black—M1 and M2

These pins provide power to the motor. The maximum voltage is the voltage of the batteries (9V for standard batteries, 7.2V for NiMH batteries). The motor is controlled by a circuit called an H-bridge (IC drivers LB1836M and LB1930M). An H-bridge is made from four transistors, and in the following figures the transistors are labeled 1 through 4.

The control circuit is designed so that transistors 1 and 2 on one side and 3 and 4 on the other side are not simultaneously conducting, to avoid shorting supply. Figure 3-3 shows the state of the transistors for going forward, with transistors 1 and 4 on. Figure 3-4 shows reverse with 2 and 3 on. Figures 3-5 and 3-6 illustrate the current flow for the brake and floating states.

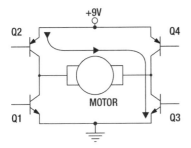

Figure 3-3. *Forward state*

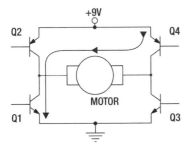

Figure 3-4. *Back state*

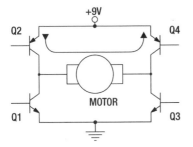

Figure 3-5. *Brake state*

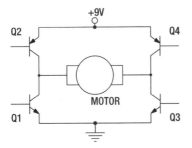

Figure 3-6. *Floating state*

The speed of the motor is controlled by pulse width modulation (PWM), as shown on the diagram in Figure 3-7. The motor power is rapidly turned on and off over a time interval. The speed of a motor depends on the average voltage applied to it, and the PWM method is a way of controlling this average voltage. It's energy efficient because the transistors are either completely off or on.

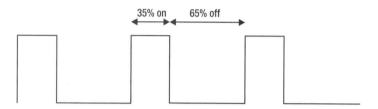

Figure 3-7. *PWM for motor at power level 35%*

With the standard firmware, the length of the cycle is 128μs. This corresponds to a 7800Hz frequency, which is an audible frequency that can sometimes be heard as a high-pitched whistling. The 128μs length of cycle allows a much better linearity of the command than the one used by the RCX. For the NXT, the relationship between the speed and the applied voltage is linear. We'll describe it further in Chapter 12. The available current on output ports is approximately 700 mA, and can attain 1A in peak. The driver has a thermal protection that limits the current when it's overheating.

Pin 3—Red—GND

This is the ground pin. Unlike the pins of the sensors, the pins 2 and 3 for the motor aren't connected together. If a sensor is accidentally connected to a motor port, the driver is partially short-circuited. The driver is well protected, but we advise you to avoid this kind of situation.

Pin 4—Green—4.3V POWER

This pin is connected to the 4.3V power supply that's shared between all the ports of the NXT.

Pin 5 and 6—Yellow and Blue—TACHO0 and TACHO1

The two inputs are used for the optical encoder built into the NXT motors. The encoder generates signals in quadrature, and that allows the NXT to determine the direction and speed of the motor. The two signals are shifted rectangular pulses, and the shift represents one quarter of phase; hence the term quadrature. Figure 3-8 illustrates the signals for a motor turning forward, and Figure 3-9 is for reverse. The frequency of the signal gives the rotational speed of the motor. One-half cycle of the signal corresponds to one degree of rotation of the motor.

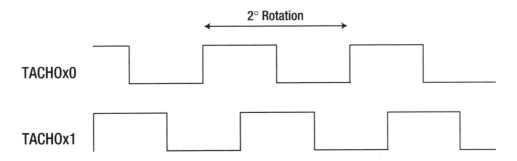

Figure 3-8. *Quadrature signals for motor running forward*

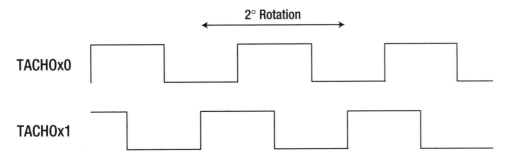

Figure 3-9. *Quadrature signals for motor running backward*

Physically Connecting to the NXT

The NXT port plugs are similar to RJ-12 modular telephone connectors with six contacts. However, the lock of the cable is on the side of the connector, instead of the middle, for a standard RJ-12. At the time of writing, we know of no provider for these connectors. Note that there are connectors, known as DEC connectors, that also have a side lock, but it's on the wrong side of the connector. Figure 3-10 illustrates an NXT cable and a standard RJ-12.

Figure 3-10. *NXT cable and standard RJ-12 cable*

Making Your Connectors

If the LEGO cables aren't available or if you want to make your own, you can modify a RJ-12 plug as explained in the following sections. However, be careful when choosing the cables to modify. The RJ-12 cables have six conductors on six positions, while RJ-11 cables (standard telephone cables) have four conductors on six positions, RJ-9 cables have four conductors on four positions, and RJ-45 (standard network cables) have eight conductors on eight positions (see Figure 3-11). There's no need to buy already-made RJ-12 cables. You can also buy some cable and connectors, and crimp them yourself using a low-cost tool.

Figure 3-11. *These connectors are not suited for NXT modification*

Taped Connector Method

For this method, you remove the latch and its support by filing, as shown in Figures 3-12 and 3-13. Then you must wrap the plug into some cellophane tape so that it fits tightly in the NXT connector. This operation is illustrated in Figure 3-14. The sides and the top must be covered, but obviously not the bottom that contains the contacts. The method is simple, but not very reliable, because there is no lock and it can be easily pulled out.

Figure 3-12. *Filing off the latch*

Figure 3-13. *Filing off the front support*

Figure 3-14. *The connector is thickened with tape*

Modified Telephone Plug Method

One of the authors (Philo) pioneered the RJ-12 surgery method. The latch is cut, trimmed, and reglued at the right place. The sliced RJ-12 connector is shown in Figure 3-15. This method is more delicate, but the connectors are more reliable. You can find a complete how-to on Philo's website: `http://philohome.com/nxtplug/nxtplug.htm`.

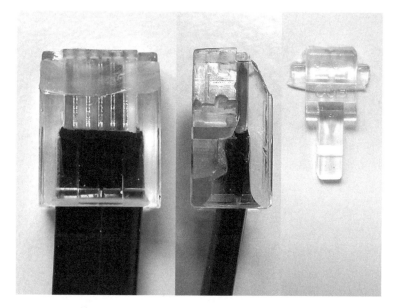

Figure 3-15. *Sliced RJ-12 connector*

Cut Cable Method

By far the easiest way to connect to the NXT is to order extra cables and just cut them in half. That gives you the plugs you need for two homebrew projects. The cable jacket is rather tough and must be cut with care so you don't cut the insulation on the wires inside. Here are the step-by-step instructions:

1. Strip 2" (5cm) of the black jacket with a sharp knife, as illustrated in Figure 3-16. Be very careful not to hurt yourself and not to damage the underlying wires. Once stripped, the NXT cable contains six colored wires; in the photo in Figure 3-17, from left to right, they are blue, yellow, green, red, black, and white.

Figure 3-16. *Cut cable method step 1: Cut the sheath.*

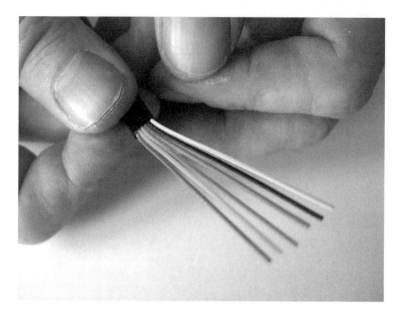

Figure 3-17. *Cut cable method: Remove the jacket.*

2. Strip all the wires, or only the ones you need if your sensor only uses a few of them. This operation is illustrated in Figure 3-18.

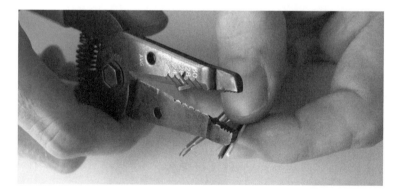

Figure 3-18. *Cut cable method step 2: Strip the individual wires.*

3. If you want to terminate the cable with a terminal block, fold down the color wire ends so that it looks like Figure 3-19. Inserting some insulator along with copper under the terminal screw provides some strain relief and avoids wire breakage.

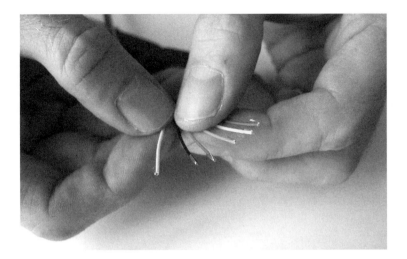

Figure 3-19. *Cut cable method step 3: Fold wire back on insulation.*

4. Screw the wires in the screw terminal as shown in Figure 3-20. The first part of the cable should look like Figure 3-21.

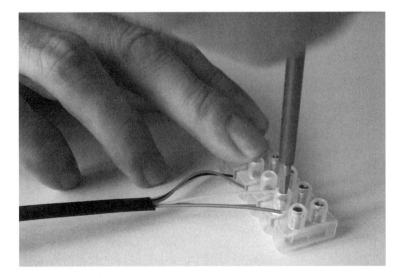

Figure 3-20. *Cut cable method step 4: Screw the cable.*

Figure 3-21. *Cut cable method step 5: All wires screwed in the terminal block*

5. Now you can connect any type of wire you need (see Figure 3-22) to extend the cable or connect it to a homebrew sensor. You should use solid wire to connect the cable to a solderless breadboard for projects described in later chapters. Appendix A describes the details for this construction method.

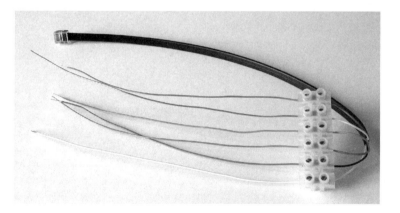

Figure 3-22. *The finished screw terminal breakout box*

Screw Terminal for Passive Sensors

This is a simplified version to be used for building sensors that only need a few of the pins. For example, only pins 1 and 2 (white and black wires) are used for sensors in Chapters 4 through 7. You can use a three-contact screw terminal to get a spare connection point, as illustrated in Figure 3-23.

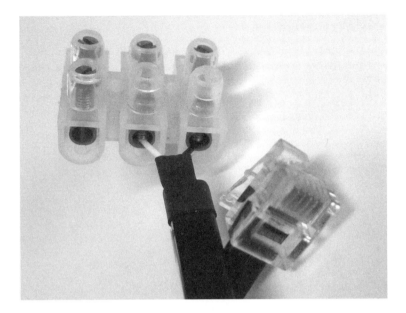

Figure 3-23. *Screw terminal cable for passive sensor prototyping*

The use of the spare connection point can be seen in this Temperature Sensor (described in Chapter 5) shown in Figure 3-24.

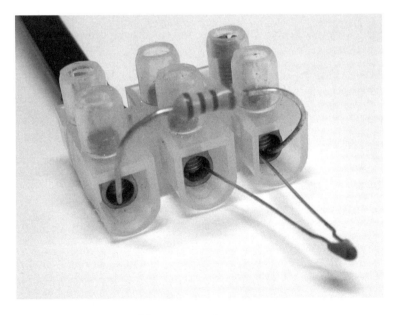

Figure 3-24. *Prototype of Temperature Sensor*

RCX Compatibility Cable

LEGO provides an RCX-compatible cable for the NXT. It allows using the RCX motors and sensors with the NXT. You can make your own with an NXT cable and an RCX cable. The compatibility cable connects a 9V RCX cable to wires 1 and 2 of an NXT cable. We'll describe how to make one with a screw terminal. You can see the different elements needed for a homebrew compatibility cable in Figure 3-25.

Figure 3-25. *Elements needed to build a compatibility cable*

1. Split the two wires of the RCX cable and strip them.

2. Fold the ends of the cables before screwing them in the terminal.

3. Strip the black sheath of the NXT cable with a cutter and cut all color cables except the black and white ones.

4. Strip the black and the white wires of the NXT cable and fold them. The prepared cable should look like the ones in Figure 3-26.

5. Screw all the wires under the screw terminals (see Figure 3-27). Folding the ends and tightening the insulating material under the screw provides some strain relief.

Figure 3-26. *Prepared cables*

Figure 3-27. *Attaching wires to the screw terminal*

6. The final cable is illustrated in Figure 3-28: it connects an RCX motor to the NXT.

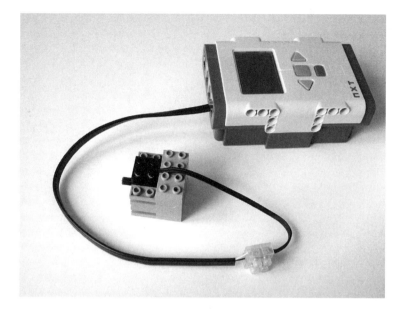

Figure 3-28. *NXT driving a 9V RCX motor*

Of course, it's also possible to make a soldered version of this cable using some heat shrink tubing to insulate and join the two sections of the cable, as shown in Figure 3-29. Figure 3-30 shows such a cable connecting an RCX Light Sensor to the NXT.

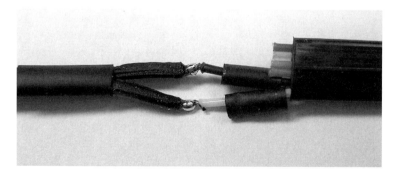

Figure 3-29. *Solder RCX and NXT wires together. Don't forget to insert heat shrink tubing!*

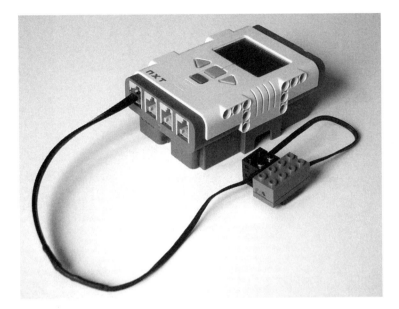

Figure 3-30. *Using an RCX Light Sensor with the NXT*

CHAPTER 4

■■■

Contact Sensors

Contact sensors are the simplest NXT sensors because they're only on or off. The LEGO Touch Sensor is a good example of a contact sensor. Homebrew contact sensors use the same NXT-G Touch Sensor block shown in Figure 4-1 as the LEGO ones. You probably already have everything you need to homebrew one. Even if you don't, the parts are readily available from electronic stores such as Radio Shack, and even from hardware stores.

Figure 4-1. *NXT-G Touch Sensor block*

We've already covered many methods for connecting to the NXT sensor inputs in Chapter 3. For contact sensors, we're interested in only two of the six connections. On the NXT plug they're pins 1 and 2, and in the cable they're the black and white wires. For now, it doesn't even matter which is which. In the examples that follow, we'll only show some 18 gauge ($0.8mm^2$) speaker wires, and you can presume they're attached to these two NXT connections.

Touching Wires

Bring up the View menu on the NXT and select the Touch Sensor on Port 1 using this sequence: NXT Menu ➤ View ➤ Touch ➤ Port 1. It should display the value 0, as in Figure 4-2. Now touch the ends of the wires together. Somehow the NXT knows you're doing that, and it changes the display to a 1, as in Figure 4-3. We know it isn't rocket science, but we can make a little game out of this.

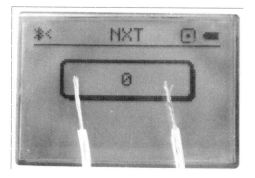

Figure 4-2. *Wires not touching reads 0.*

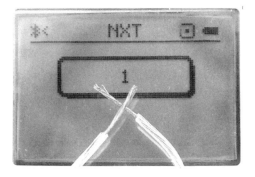

Figure 4-3. *Touching wires reads 1.*

Electronic Surfboard

Over the years this game has been called many things. "Electronic Surfboard' is the most imaginative, while "The Steady Hand Game" seems a little uninspiring. It's a dexterity game where you try to pass a small loop of wire over a second wire without touching it. To make things challenging, the second wire is bent randomly around like waves, hence the surfing theme.

Construction

Construction of the game is simple enough to figure out using only the photograph in Figure 4-4. We used heavy 12 gauge (3mm^2) house wire for the loop and waves, but you could use much lighter single-strand hook-up wire if you wanted to.

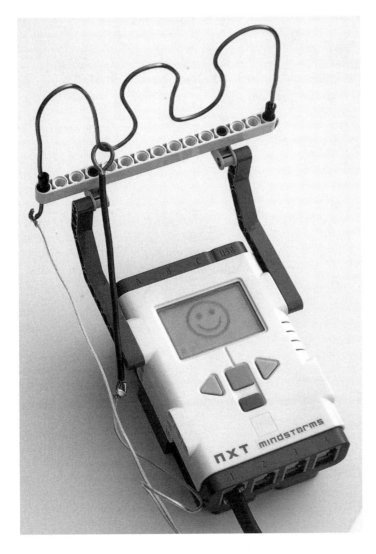

Figure 4-4. *Electronic Surfboard game*

Programming

In the elementary school version of the game, touching the wires together completes a circuit that has a buzzer in series with a battery. Our wires are connected to a 32-bit computer, so you might expect a little more than a buzz. Referring to the NXT-G program in Figure 4-5, the number of times the wires touch is counted up to a maximum limit. The display is animated, and a dramatic "Ouch" is played whenever there is a touch. Finally, if the limit of touches is reached, the "Game Over" phrase is uttered.

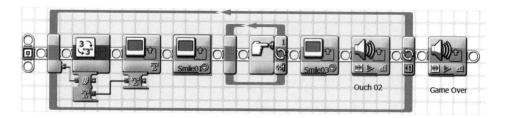

Figure 4-5. *NXT-G Surfboard game*

Switches

Switches are the workhorses of the input world. Figure 4-6 shows just a few examples of what switches look like. People turn switches on all the time to make things happen. If a room is too dark, you turn on a light with a switch. The vast majority of automated electrical control is also done with switches that change state with temperature, pressure, humidity, weight, liquid level, position, or practically anything else you can imagine. If the temperature is too cold, turn on the heat with a thermostatic switch.

Figure 4-6. *Examples of switches: pressure, temperature, rotary, micro, push button, and key*

The humble wall switch like the one in Figure 4-7 is the easiest place to start. Sure, it's overkill to use a switch capable of controlling about a thousand times the current of an NXT, but they are dirt cheap and simple to hook up. The nice thing about this type of toggle switch is that, unlike the LEGO Touch Sensor, it stays however you set it. Just connect one wire to each screw and you're ready to go.

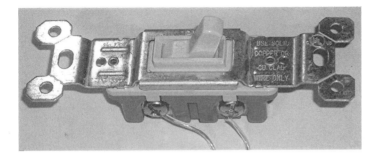

Figure 4-7. *Wall switch*

Parallel and Series

Sometimes you need more than four contact sensors for a project, but the NXT only has four inputs. In a Chapter 13 we'll cover ways to expand the number of NXT sensor inputs, but for now let's look at some simple ways to connect multiple switches to the same input.

If you connect more than one switch to the same input by connecting them in parallel as shown in Figure 4-8, then when any switch is turned on the NXT input is considered to be on. You can use this for a vehicle with bumper switches located on all four sides. Touching any one of the bumpers triggers the same avoidance reaction. You could easily make this type of connection with the old RCX by just plugging multiple switches onto the same input. The NXT connectors don't allow this, so you have to do it with wire.

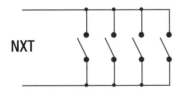

Figure 4-8. *Parallel switches on one input*

If the switches are connected in series as in Figure 4-9, then they must all be on to make the NXT input on. Typically this kind of circuit is used for applications where a unanimous vote from multiple inputs is needed to cause some important thing to happen. For example, a switch located on the bottom of each foot of a robot dog is used to make sure it has all its feet firmly planted on the ground.

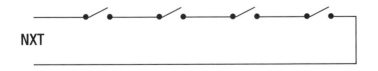

Figure 4-9. *Series switches on one input*

Antenna Sensor

You can build an antenna sensor or feeler using the same principle as the electronic surfboard game. The antenna or whisker is made from an electric guitar D string. This type of string is a thin wire that has another steel wire wound around it to make it heaver. The A and E strings also work, but their wire is thicker and stiffer, which makes a slightly less sensitive feeler. You can purchase a whole set of inexpensive guitar strings at music stores and even discount stores. One guitar string is long enough to make about five sensors. Figure 4-10 shows the NXT Quick Start Vehicle outfitted with two antenna sensors.

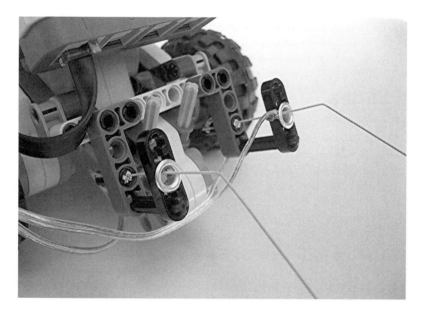

Figure 4-10. *NXT Quick Start Vehicle with feelers*

The contact ring support is a type of Technic lift arm beam that isn't included with the NXT kit. You can get this part in the Technic Beams accessory kit (PN#10072 from LEGO Shop at Home). The ring is a 3/16 inch (4.76mm) brass eyelet shown in Figure 4-11. Normally these are used to reinforce a material such as fabric or leather, where a lace or screw has to pass through it. You should be able to find these at hardware or craft supply stores.

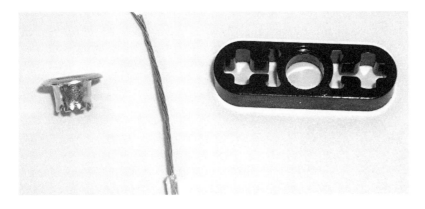

Figure 4-11. *Contact ring step 1*

Using 18 gauge speaker wire, loop it through the hole twice, as shown in Figure 4-12, and twist it on itself. This decreases the hole diameter a little and makes the eyelet fit tightly without any glue. After you press the eyelet into the hole, it will look like Figure 4-13.

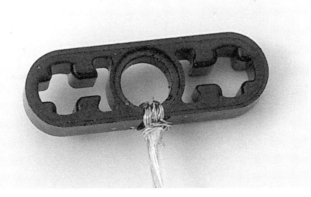

Figure 4-12. *Contact ring step 2*

Figure 4-13. *Contact ring step 3*

Use about 7 inches (18cm) of guitar wire for the antenna. Don't cut the guitar wire with your good electronic cutters; it is very hard and will probably wreck them. Use heavy-duty diagonal cutters or pliers to cut it. Bend one end of the wire into the T shape shown in Figure 4-14. The base of the antenna is made from a Technic friction pin and a little aluminum foil.

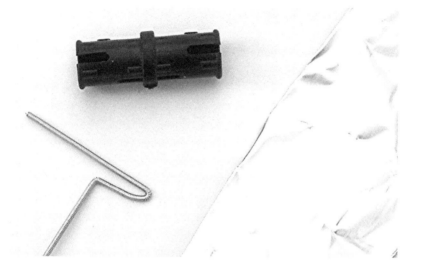

Figure 4-14. *Antenna base step 1*

Feed the antenna through one of the little slots in the side of the pin as in Figure 4-15. Work the T end so that it bridges through the slot on the other side of the pin. You can now connect the other speaker wire to the antenna through the loop in the T.

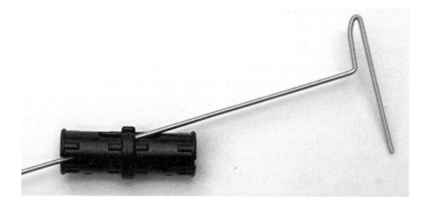

Figure 4-15. *Antenna base step 2*

Twist some Aluminum foil into a thin roll and pack it all around the wire to center it inside the pin. This also keeps it from pulling out of the pin. Your finished antenna base should look like Figure 4-16.

Figure 4-16. *Antenna base step 3*

Combine the antenna and contact ring using the Technic right angle beam and an axle assembled like Figure 4-17. The distance from the pin to the contact ring adjusts the sensitivity of the feeler. The closer the ring is to the pin, the less sensitive the feeler becomes. If you're making more than one, it's a good idea to reverse the direction of the right angle beam so you end up with two symmetrical sensors.

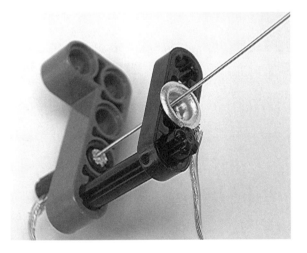

Figure 4-17. *Finished antenna sensor*

After you've mounted the antenna sensors on the vehicle, bend the antennas so they point slightly down and outward. You'll probably need to modify the construction to make them work with other robot designs. The antennas might also need to be periodically adjusted, as they get bent from use.

The sensors are connected in parallel as shown in Figure 4-18, and only use one input for the avoidance reaction. The NXT-G program is in Figure 4-19. The robot goes forward till one of the feelers touches something. Then the robot quickly reverses and turns about 90 degrees. After that it continues to go forward until it hits something again.

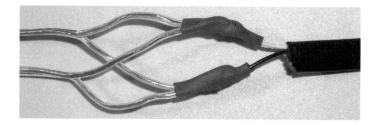

Figure 4-18. *Parallel connection of two antenna sensors*

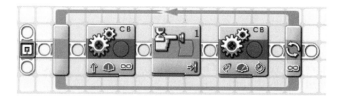

Figure 4-19. *Quick Start Vehicle with feeler program*

Going Further

In this book we try to emphasize designs that involve all new components so that you can reproduce the projects exactly as presented. However, switches are everywhere. There are two nice ones in that discarded computer mouse over there in your junk box. Recycling switches is a practical and economical way to expand your NXT's sensor inputs.

CHAPTER 5

Resistive Sensors

Resistive sensors are an example of an NXT passive-type sensor. The term passive sensor sounds like it could be an oxymoron. After all, how could anything that senses also be passive? The term is a carryover from the old RCX days when there were only two types of sensors: those that required a power supply and those that didn't. You probably figured out that passive sensors were the type that didn't. The contact sensors you learned about in Chapter 4 were also passive sensors.

Connecting a resistive sensor to the NXT is just like the contact sensor. You use only two of the six sensor input connections. On the NXT plug they're pins 1 and 2, and in the cable they're the black and white wires. It still doesn't matter which is which. In the examples that follow we'll show 18 gauge (0.8mm^2) speaker wires, and you can presume that they're attached to these two NXT connections.

Analog to Digital Conversion

There's a lot more going on inside your NXT than just what's needed to decide if a switch is on or off. The NXT uses an analog-to-digital converter to change the analog voltage between the two wires into a digital number, from 0 for 0V to 1,023 for 5V. Right about now you're probably wondering, "A switch doesn't make voltage, so how is the NXT going to convert anything?" Inside the NXT a 10kΩ resistor is permanently connected from pin 1 (or the white wire in the cable) to 5V. Pin 2 (or the black wire in the cable) is permanently connected to ground or 0V. Figure 5-1 is a diagram of the internal circuitry.

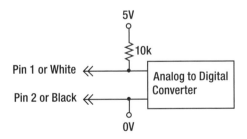

Figure 5-1. *NXT sensor input*

If all you have is a switch hooked up to the input as in Figure 5-2, the input is either pulled up to 5V when the switch is off or 0V when it is on. Those are the extremes, but if the connection is somewhere between open and shorted you get a voltage somewhere between 0V and 5V and a converter value between 0 and 1,023. This is what happens when you connect a resistor to the input, as in Figure 5-3.

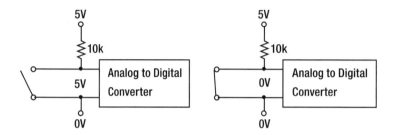

Figure 5-2. *Open and closed switch input*

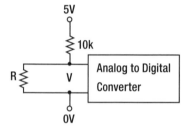

Figure 5-3. *Resistor input*

A circuit with two resistors in series is called a voltage divider because the voltage across both of them is divided in the middle. How the voltage is divided depends on the values of the resistors. This equation describes the voltage across the external resistor R, where the 10,000 comes from the 10kΩ resistor inside the NXT and the 5 is from the 5V supply:

$$V = \frac{R}{10,000 + R} \ 5 \ \ [V]$$

The NXT analog-to-digital converter scales the voltage to what are called Raw units. The 1,023 comes from the fact that the converter has 10 bits of accuracy, and 1,023 is the biggest number you can express with 10 bits:

$$Raw = \frac{1023}{5} V$$

When the NXT thinks it's connected to a switch, it compares the Raw value to 460. If the input value is greater, it takes the input to be open, and if it's less it is closed. The Raw value is available in NXT-G by using the expanded Touch Sensor block shown in Figure 5-4. The lowest terminal with the 10101010 next to it outputs the Raw value.

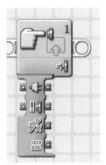

Figure 5-4. *Expanded Touch Sensor*

Ohmmeter

I know you can buy a good digital Ohmmeter for a fraction of the cost of an NXT, but sometimes it's handy to know the resistance of whatever you have connected to the input. With a little algebra, you can write an equation that converts Raw values into the value of the external resistor R:

$$R = \frac{10,000 \;\; \text{Raw}}{1023\text{-Raw}} \quad [\Omega]$$

Ohmmeter Program

Creating an NXT-G program to display the resistance is straightforward. All you need to do is read the input and run the Raw value through the equation, as illustrated in Figure 5-5. The smallest resistance value displayed greater than 0 is 9Ω, and the biggest value is 1,022,000Ω. That's a pretty wide range.

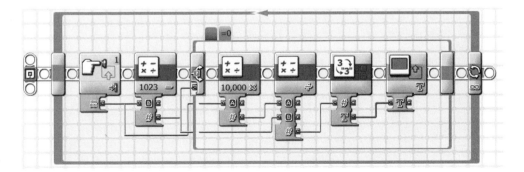

Figure 5-5. *Ohmmeter program*

One little problem occurs when the input isn't connected to anything, and the Raw value becomes 1,023. That results in a division by 0, which is correctly infinity, but the NXT doesn't do infinity. It just gives up and outputs a value of 0. For that single case, Figure 5-6 shows how the NXT-G program displays the word "Infinity."

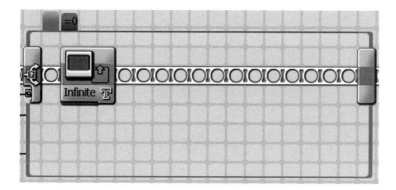

Figure 5-6. *Ohmmeter program special open-circuit case*

Measuring Salinity

As long as you've made an Ohmmeter, you might as well use it for something scientific. Salinity is an important water-quality measurement because plants and animals can't tolerate a lot of salt in their water. The more salt dissolved in water, the more conductive or less resistive it becomes. It's remarkable how little salt it takes to drop the resistance in half.

Stick the two bare ends of the wires into a flask of clean water as shown in Figure 5-7 and note the resistance. Ideally pure water will have infinite resistance, but tap water will probably show some resistance. Carefully, without moving the distance between the wires, add a few grains of salt. Wait for it to dissolve entirely and note the resistance. Repeat this process till you have a plot of resistance and concentration, as in Figure 5-8. Then you can use the plot backwards to determine the salinity given the resistance of an unknown sample.

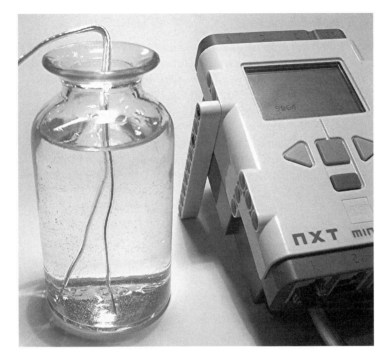

Figure 5-7. *Measuring the salinity of water*

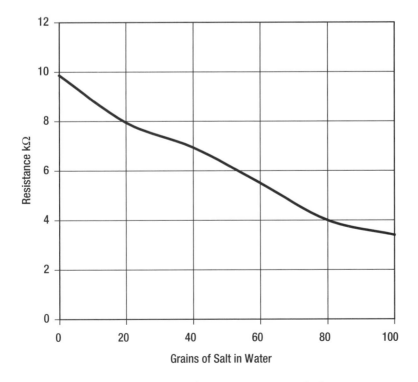

Figure 5-8. *Resistance of water with varying amounts of salt*

Temperature Sensor

Temperature is one of the most useful measurements you can make with your NXT. You can use the NXT as a digital thermometer to monitor the temperature of an experiment continuously, or you can log the temperature into a file to see how the value has changed over a long time period. You can even use the value in a control loop that regulates temperature.

LEGO makes a Temperature Sensor as pictured in Figure 5-9 (PN#W979889). It is a legacy sensor from the RCX and requires the NXT conversion cable (PN#770323) or one you make yourself. It's a little expensive, considering you can build your own for about one-tenth the price. The LEGO sensor isn't suitable for every sensing application anyway. For example, I wouldn't use it to monitor the temperature inside a hamster cage. The hamster might mistake it for a chew toy.

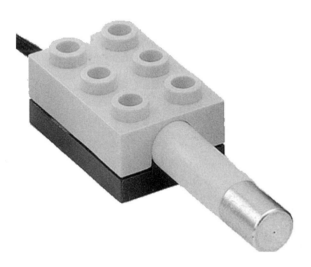

Figure 5-9. *LEGO Temperature Sensor*

The temperature-measuring range of the NXT is from –4°F to 158°F, or –20°C to 70°C. LEGO probably didn't want you to boil your temperature probe. Although limited, it still represents a decent range of temperatures you're likely to encounter.

Thermistors

The LEGO Temperature Sensor is based on an electronic component called a thermistor, like those illustrated in Figure 5-10. A thermistor is an unusual resistor that changes resistance value with temperature. The name *thermistor* is just the combination of the two words thermal and resistor. The particular thermistor used with the NXT decreases in resistance with an increase in temperature. Because the slope of the relationship between temperature and resistance is negative, the type is known as a Negative Temperature Coefficient or NTC thermistor.

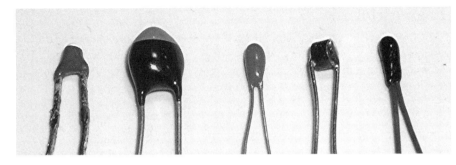

Figure 5-10. *Examples of thermistors, with the GE RL0503-5820-97-MS on the right*

A thermistor is manufactured by attaching two wires to a tiny pellet of semiconducting material, which is usually a metallic oxide (see Figure 5-11). When the temperature of the pellet increases, more electrons in the semiconductor are made available to conduct electricity, so the resistance goes down. Usually the whole thing is coated with epoxy to seal it from moisture and other contamination. Variations in the room temperature resistance and the amount that the resistance changes with temperature create hundreds of different thermistors to choose from. Additionally, size, packaging, and accuracy take the selection well into the thousands.

Figure 5-11. *Semiconducting pellet inside a thermistor*

Reverse Engineering the NXT

How do we find a thermistor compatible with the NXT? We start by reverse engineering the NXT Raw-to-temperature-conversion equation. The plot in Figure 5-12 was made by recording both the temperature and Raw values simultaneously. As you can see, the NXT conversion equation isn't a simple offset or multiplier.

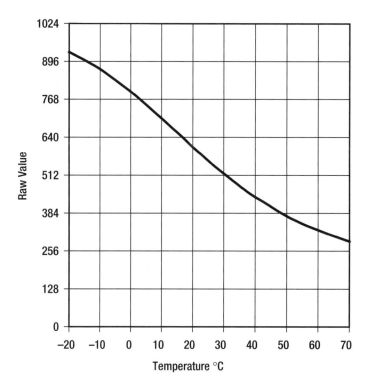

Figure 5-12. *Plot of temperature and Raw value*

You already know how to convert a Raw value into a resistance measurement from the NXT Ohmmeter project. Feeding Raw values into the equation and calculating R values allows you to make a plot of temperature and sensor resistance, as in Figure 5-13. You must match this plot for an NXT-compatible Temperature Sensor.

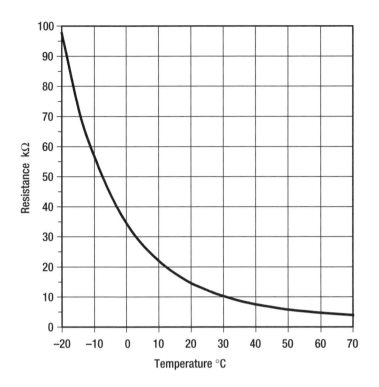

Figure 5-13. *NXT Temperature Sensor resistance plot*

You can compute the resistance value of any thermistor by a rather complex equation, where β is related to the shape of the curve and R_{25} is the resistance at 25°C. The two parameters β and R_{25} are all that's needed to thermoelectrically define a thermistor:

$$R = R_{25} \exp\left[\frac{\beta(25 - T)}{(T + 273.15)(298.15)}\right] \Omega$$

The value for R_{25} from the NXT Temperature Sensor plot is 12.2kΩ. This is a big problem, because no commercially available thermistor has an R_{25} of 12.2kΩ. The closest value is 10kΩ. So LEGO must have put a 2.2kΩ resistor in series with the thermistor for some reason. We'll spare you the painful details, but the β value can be determined by a least squares regression between the equation and the NXT plot. The value turns out to be 3,750, or a temperature coefficient of –4.22%/°C @25°C.

The good news is that you can buy a thermistor just like this with an R_{25} of 10kΩ and a β of 3,750. It's the GE Infrastructure Sensing type NHQM103B375T10. The bad news is that it's a tiny surface-mount chip to which you can't easily make connections. There are a lot of thermistors with an R_{25} of 10kΩ, but their β values are a little different.

Probably just to make life interesting, not all supply catalogs print values for β. Instead they give an equivalent temperature coefficient expressed as %/°C @25°C, which is usually a negative number around five. You can just multiply the temperature coefficient by –888 to convert it to β. Occasionally you'll see a Resistance Ratio, which is the resistance at 0°C divided by the resistance at 50°C. You can convert this to a β too, with an equation where *ln* is the natural log function. If you work the equation backward, it turns out that the NXT thermistor Ratio should be 8.37.

$$\beta = \frac{\ln(Ratio)}{.0005665}$$

A thermistor with a β of 3,907 or temperature coefficient of –4.4%/°C would have less than 1/2°C error over most of the temperature range you're likely to be measuring, and barely a degree at the extremes, as shown in Figure 5-14. That thermistor is a GE Infrastructure Sensing type RL0503-5820-97MS, which can be purchased from Digi-Key (PN# KC003T-ND.) It features good accuracy, insulated leads, and is reasonably priced.

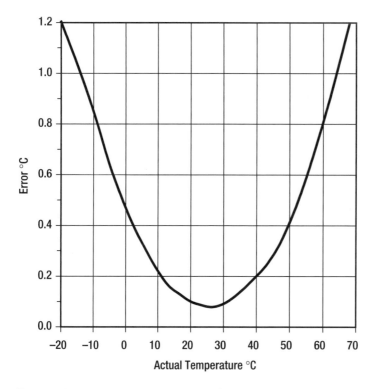

Figure 5-14. *Temperature error using a thermistor with β = 3907*

Homebrew Temperature Sensor

Making the thermistor into an NXT Temperature Sensor requires a little soldering and heat shrink tubing. We need to put a 2.2kΩ resistor in series with the thermistor to make it look just like the LEGO Temperature Sensor to the NXT. In addition to different values of resistance, resistors come in different sizes to accommodate heat generated by the part. Quarter- and half-watt values are the most common for leaded parts. The power levels are insignificant in this case, so we'll use the quarter-watt size. Resistors also come with different accuracies, with 1% and 5% most common. A 5% will do just fine, so the color-coded bands on the resistor should read red-red-red-gold. Figure 5-15 shows all the components you need except the heat shrink tubing.

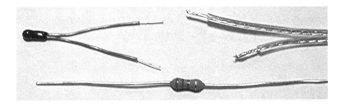

Figure 5-15. *Homebrew Temperature Sensor step 1*

After cutting the leads of the resistor and stripping the wire to about 3/16" (4mm) as shown in Figure 5-16, solder the thermocouple, resistor, and wire as shown. Don't forget to slide the heat shrink tubing on first! Watch that you don't heat the tubing up with the soldering iron and shrink it before you want to.

Figure 5-16. *Homebrew Temperature Sensor step 2*

After soldering, slide the heat shrink tubing over the joints and shrink using a hair dryer. You should end up with something like Figure 5-17.

Figure 5-17. *Homebrew Temperature Sensor step 3*

Shrinking a large piece of tubing over the whole assembly, as in Figure 5-18, protects it and gives it a more "finished" look.

Figure 5-18. *Finished Homebrew Temperature Sensor*

Depending on how you intend to use your Temperature Sensor, you might need to package it further. An easy way to waterproof the sensor is to slip it into one of those long skinny balloons clowns twist up to make animals (see Figure 5-19). You also could put it into a metal tube to guard it from hamster teeth.

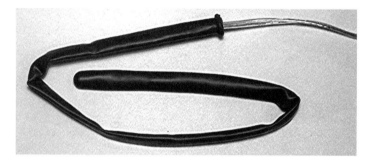

Figure 5-19. *Waterproofed Temperature Sensor*

NXT Digital Thermometer

The easiest way to use your Temperature Sensor is with the NXT View menu using the following sequence: NXT menu ➤ View ➤ Select Temperature C ➤ Port 1. This turns the NXT into a digital thermometer. The thermistor has very little mass, and you'll be amazed how fast the temperature changes by just pinching the Temperature Sensor between your fingers.

A quick way to check the calibration of your new Temperature Sensor is to submerse it in a mixture of crushed ice and a little water. You definitely need to use a balloon to waterproof the sensor, as illustrated in Figure 5-20. Poke a channel through the ice with something like a pencil, and insert the sensor into the middle. After a few minutes, the NXT should read a temperature just a little above freezing, such as 0.5°C.

Figure 5-20. *NXT digital thermometer using the View menu*

Adding some salt to the ice water mixture forces some of the ice to melt. As it does, it absorbs heat, and the temperature of the water drops. We only put in a tablespoon of salt and the temperature dropped more than 8°C, like the display in Figure 5-21. You can approach a temperature of −20°C this way.

Figure 5-21. *Temperature of ice and salt water*

Relative Humidity Sensor

Relative humidity is a measure of how much moisture is in the air. One hundred percent means you can't get more water into the air, so it must very damp. Zero percent is totally dry, and must be in a desert somewhere. People are only comfortable within a range of temperatures and humidities. The plot in Figure 5-22 shows the comfort zone for an average person in both the winter and summer. In the summer you can see that the humidity must only be 50% to be comfortable at 27°C (81°F).

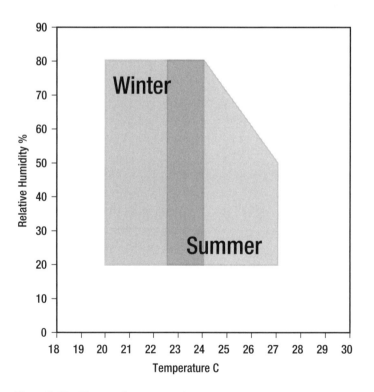

Figure 5-22. *The comfort zone*

One way to measure the relative humidity is to make two temperature measurements. One directly of the air is called the dry bulb temperature (Tdry), and the other temperature is of a wet object—the wet bulb temperature (Twet). You can then use the dry bulb temperature and the difference between it and the wet bulb temperature (DeltaT) to look up the relative humidity in a table or calculate it from a formula.

Figure 5-23 shows how to measure the wet bulb temperature. The Temperature Sensor only extends to about the lip of the jar. The rest of the absorbent material wrapped around it supplies water from the vial to keep the sensor wet. Don't submerge the sensor into the water, or you'll read a temperature that's warmer than the wet bulb.

Figure 5-23. *Wet bulb Temperature Sensor*

The humidity calculation is related to the ratio of vapor pressures of water at the two temperatures, plus other factors such as air pressure. They're rather complex, and the NXT doesn't have the math capability to implement them. Instead, you can use a simplified equation that won't have more than 5% error over the range you're likely to be measuring. The equation expects the temperatures to be in Celsius:

$$H = 100 - \frac{244\,(\text{Tdry-Twet})}{(\text{Tdry}+12)} \quad [\%]$$

The NXT-G snippet shows the equation converted to code as a My Block in Figure 5-24. Because NXT-G only uses integer arithmetic, the multiplication by 244 needs to be done before the divide. You also need to divide the values from Temperature blocks by ten before passing them to the humidity My Block because the NXT scales the temperatures up by a factor of ten. Remember to set the Temperature block for Celsius too.

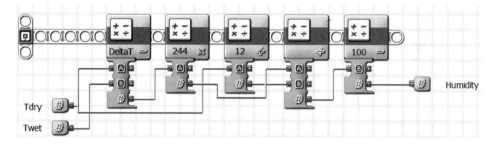

Figure 5-24. *Relative humidity My Block*

Light Sensor

You're probably saying, "I already have a perfectly good Light Sensor." Is your sensor's sensitivity to wavelength the same as the human eye? Is it smaller than a pencil eraser? Does it have an extremely broad operating range and can be purchased for less than $2? Not if you're talking about the NXT Light Sensor. Also, what if your project needs more than one Light Sensor? The Cadmium Sulfide CdS photocell or Light Dependent Resistor (LDR) is a good alternative to the NXT Light Sensor.

LDRs vary in resistance over a wide range of values, from about 1,000 ohms in bright daylight to millions of ohms in total darkness. They are made from a ceramic disk with two electrodes plated on the face that have a thin gap between them. The gap between the electrodes is maximized in length by making it into a serpentine shape that can be seen through the layer of photoresistive, in this case CdS, material painted on the surface.

A large variety of CdS LDRs are commercially available, such as those in Figure 5-25. They differ primarily in the operating resistance range and package size. All of them work with the NXT to some extent, but when buying individual devices, look for a bright light resistance such as 3kΩ. This maximizes the range of values the NXT can convert given the internal 10kΩ pull-up resistor. Don't worry about characteristics such as voltage or wattage. Also, don't confuse photocells with solar cells, which actually generate voltage from light.

Figure 5-25. *Examples of CdS photoresistors or Light Dependent Resistors (LDRs)*

Building the Light Sensor

The easiest way to build your own Light Sensor is to purchase an assortment of five LDRs from Radio Shack (276-1657). If there are several packages in the store to pick from, get an assortment that has at least two that look exactly the same. This pair will come in handy for projects that need equally matched sensors. The other approach is to buy some specific LDRs; then you know exactly what you're going to get.

The Selco Products plastic-coated type 8P are ideal LDRs for the NXT, in particular the model 8001 (Digi-Key PDV-P8001-ND). These LDRs have a low cell resistance in bright light, and the 5.08mm diameter is also compatible with the Technic hole size for easy mounting.

Start by stripping the connecting wires and clipping the leads of the LDR to about 3/16 inch (4mm). Make sure you slide some heat shrink tubing over the wires before you solder the connections, as shown in Figure 5-26.

Figure 5-26. *Homebrew Light Sensor step 1*

Twist the wires around the LDR leads and solder them to look like Figure 5-27.

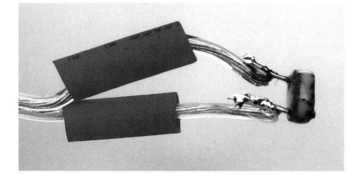

Figure 5-27. *Homebrew Light Sensor step 2*

Push the tubing tight to the LDR and shrink it with a hair dryer. Your sensor should look like Figure 5-28.

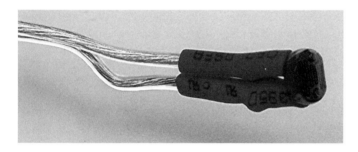

Figure 5-28. *Homebrew Light Sensor step 3*

Slide an additional piece of heat shrink tubing over both wires to additionally strain-relief the connections. Now your sensor should look like Figure 5-29.

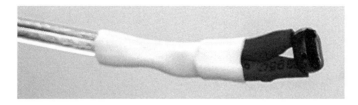

Figure 5-29. *Homebrew Light Sensor step 4*

Run the connecting wires through the hole in the Technic right angle beam, as shown in Figure 5-30. Using a friction pin and a blue axle pin, sandwich the photocell with a 3-hole beam. This beam holds the LDR in place and makes the light sensitivity of the sensor more directional.

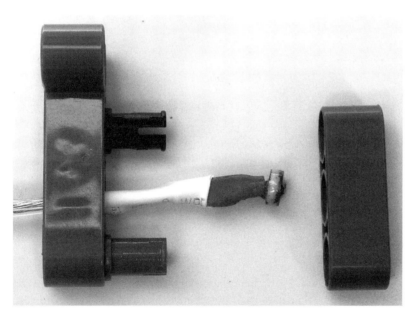

Figure 5-30. *Homebrew Light Sensor assembly*

Your finished Light Sensor should look like Figure 5-31. When you're making more than one of these, it's a good idea to reverse the direction of the right angle beam. That way you end up with two symmetrical sensors.

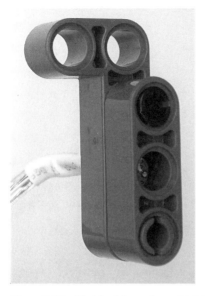

Figure 5-31. *Finished homebrew Light Sensor*

Comparison of LEGO and CdS Light Sensor

The resistance of a CdS LDR drops with light level, just like the NTC thermistor resistance changes with temperature, and for the same reason. Probably not all LDRs work this way, but you can model the resistance of the type 8P sensors with a simple equation. For the 8001 the value of K is 10,000:

$$R = \frac{K}{\sqrt{Lux}} \ [\Omega]$$

Humans experience light levels over a huge range in the course of a day. Table 5-1 shows that light variation from starlight to sunlight is a variation from 0.001 to 100,000 lux. The resistance of the CdS sensor over a somewhat more limited range is shown in the plot in Figure 5-32. The light level axis has to be plotted with a logarithmic scale to allow for the wide range of values.

Table 5-1. *Typical Light Levels*

Light	Lux
Daylight	50,000–100,000
Hazy	25,000–50,000
Cloudy bright	10,000–25,000
Store windows	1,000–5,000
Office	200–500
Living room	50–200
Hallway	50–100
Street lights	1–20
Full moon	0.01–0.2
Starlight	0.001

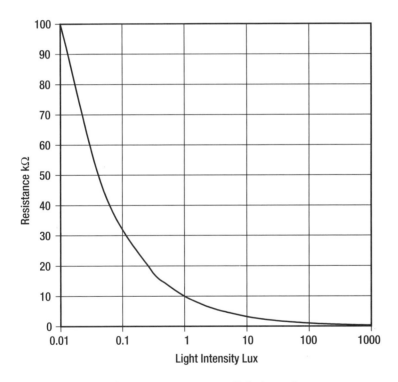

Figure 5-32. *Plot of LDR resistance versus light intensity*

Using the resistance equation for the 8001 LDR, a Raw value can be predicted for the sensor at various light levels and plotted in Figure 5-33. Unlike the NXT Light Sensor, the Raw value decreases with increasing light. The Raw values vary over a range from almost 0 to more than 900. The CdS sensor also varies more at low light level than the NXT, and continues to vary after the NXT sensor hits 100 in bright light. The biggest disadvantage of the CdS sensor over the NXT sensor is that it changes value much more slowly.

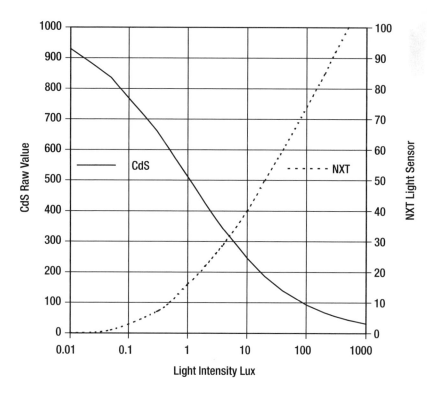

Figure 5-33. *CdS and NXT Light Sensor comparison*

Theremin

The theremin was named after Léon Theremin, who invented it in 1919. It was probably the first all-electronic musical instrument, and Figure 5-34 shows Léon playing it. It was played by a musician merely waving his hands around the instrument without ever touching it. The distance of the right hand to a vertical antenna controlled the pitch or frequency of the note, while the distance of the left hand to a loop antenna controlled the volume. It produces an eerie monotone that was popular in 1950s science fiction films.

Figure 5-34. *Inventor Léon Theremin playing his theremin*

The original theremin used radio waves to detect the placement of the musician's hands. The NXT theremin uses the amount of light falling on two homebrew Light Sensors. The sensors are mounted on arms extending from the sides of the NXT, as shown in Figure 5-35. While playing, you need to arrange the light so your hands cast shadows onto the sensors. The closer you hold your hand to the sensor, the darker the shadow.

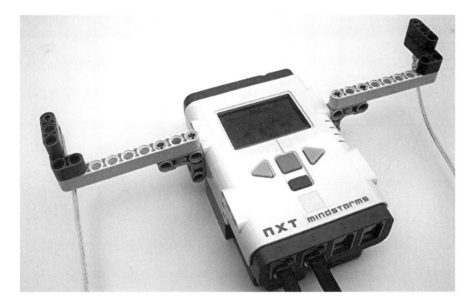

Figure 5-35. *NXT theremin*

The NXT-G program shown in Figure 5-36 couldn't be much simpler. The Raw value from the volume sensor is read in on port 1. To make sure the value reaches 0 or less, the first math block subtracts 400 from the Raw value. The next math block scales the value to the range of the volume input on the sound block. You might need to adjust these values for your particular sensors and lighting conditions. The sound block volume input range is 0 to 100, but it actually only has five volume levels: 100, 75, 50, 25, and 0 for mute. Unfortunately, this coarse volume control limits the vibrato effects the original theremin is famous for. The tone or pitch is read in on port 2, and can be fed directly to the tone input of the sound block.

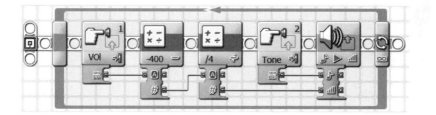

Figure 5-36. *NXT-G theremin program*

Moving your hand toward the volume Light Sensor increases the volume, while moving your other hand toward the tone Light Sensor increases the frequency of the note. A unique feature of a theremin is that it can hold a note indefinitely if you don't move either hand.

Braitenberg Vehicle 2

In the book *Vehicles: Experiments in Synthetic Psychology* (The MIT Press, 1986), Valentino Braitenberg wrote about the dynamic behavior of several minimalistic vehicles. Despite their simple design and control, their behavior was often complex and unexpected. Figure 5-37 shows his vehicle number 2. It has two photo sensors in the front that point forward, and two motor-driven wheels in the rear. Model 2a's control is arranged so that the brighter the light shining on a photo sensor, the faster the motor turns on the same side. Model 2b has the control signals crossed.

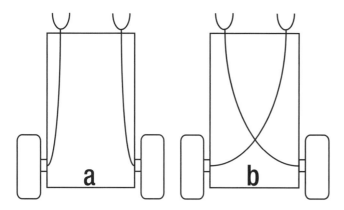

Figure 5-37. *Braitenberg vehicles Number 2a and b*

Vehicle Number 2 is easy to reproduce with the NXT Quick Start Vehicle and two home-brew Light Sensors. They can just hang down from the horizontal beam in the front, much like the feelers from Chapter 4, as illustrated in Figure 5-38.

Figure 5-38. *NXT Quick Start robot with Light Sensors*

The NXT-G program in Figure 5-39 is an endless loop that reads the two Light Sensors and adjusts the power to the two motors. Because the homebrew Light Sensor's Raw value decreases with increasing light level, the first math block subtracts the Raw value from 1,000. This makes a value that's larger with brighter light. The second math block divides the number by 10 to scale it into the 0-to-100 range used for the power input to the motor block. All you need to change between the 2a and 2b vehicles' programs is the motor designator letters B and C.

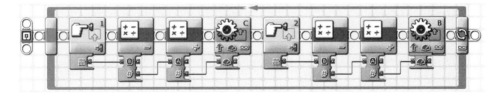

Figure 5-39. *Vehicle 2b NXT-G program*

Suppose model 2a is in a dark room, and a bright light that's in front and to the right of the vehicle is turned on, as in Figure 5-40. The right photo sensor receives more light than the left, and therefore the right motor turns faster than the left. This causes the vehicle to go forward but turn to the left, avoiding the light source. The vehicle behaves like it "hates" light.

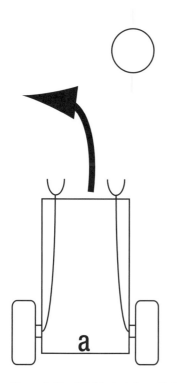

Figure 5-40. *Vehicle 2a's hate light behavior*

Now suppose model 2b is exposed to the same bright light, as in Figure 5-41. Again the right photo sensor receives more light than the left, but this time the left motor turns faster. This causes the vehicle to move forward but turn to the right seeking the light source. The vehicle behaves like it "loves" the light.

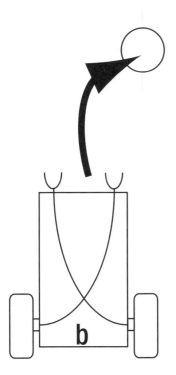

Figure 5-41. *Vehicle 2b's love light behavior*

Two Switch Input

One problem with the parallel and series methods already covered is that you can't tell which switch is being operated. An easy way to make the switches identifiable is to put a unique resistor in series with them. Figure 5-42 shows the schematic diagram of the concept.

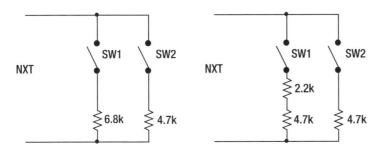

Figure 5-42. *Two versions of the two switch multiplexer*

Figure 5-43 shows the Raw values for all four of the possible switch combinations. If neither switch is closed, the NXT reads a Raw value of 1,023. If only switch one (SW1) is closed, the voltage divider is the 10k of the NXT and the 6.8k resistor. The NXT will read this as a Raw value of 414. If only switch two (SW2) is closed, the voltage divider has a 4.7k in place of the 6.8k, and this will be read as a Raw value of 327. Finally, if both switches are closed, then the voltage divider has the parallel combination of the 4.7k and 6.8k, which is 2.8k. This will be read as a Raw value of 222.

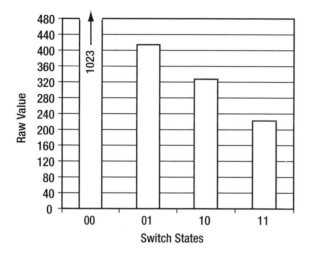

Figure 5-43. *Values for the different combinations of switches*

In theory, you could extend this concept to even more switches and resistors. However, the decoding process gets more complex, and the tolerance for variations in the resistors gets smaller. Besides, in Chapter 13 we'll really show you ways to expand the inputs.

The values of the two resistors are important. If you use resistors that are too different, the Raw values won't end up in the right place for the decoding process to work. The 4.7k resistor is easy to get at Radio Shack in a package of 5 or in a big assortment kit. The 5% color code is yellow-blue-red-gold. The 6.8k (5% color code: green-violet-red-gold) resistor is harder to find. However, you can use another 4.7k and a 2.2k (5% color code: red-red-red-gold) in series to create a 6.9k resistor, and this will still work without any adjustments to the program.

Building a Two Switch Input

Building the two switch input is easy. In step one, shown in Figure 5-44, solder the resistors to the switch and interconnect wires. Remember to have a short piece of shrink tubing to slide over the terminal without a resistor. Shrink the short piece of tubing and then slide a long piece of tubing over the wire to cover all the connections. Naturally your switches don't have to be right next to each other like the ones in the photograph. They could be on the front and back of a robot to detect that it has driven or backed into something.

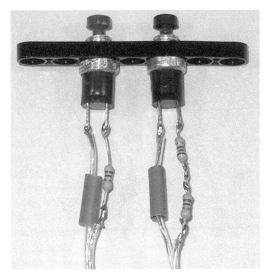

Figure 5-44. *Two switch step 1*

After soldering, slide the heat shrink tubing up to the switch and shrink it with a hair dryer. It should look like Figure 5-45.

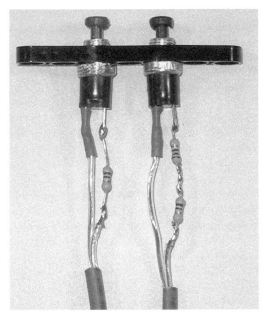

Figure 5-45. *Two switch step 2*

Finally, shrink a piece of tubing over all the connections and resistors. Your finished two-switch input will look like Figure 5-46.

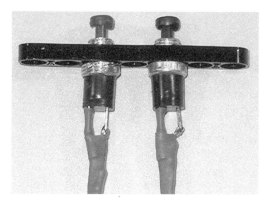

Figure 5-46. *Two switch step 3*

Programming a Two Switch Input

An NXT-G My Block shown in Figure 5-47 sorts out the four switch combinations by comparing the incoming Raw value with levels that are in between the switch states. The state of SW2 is easy to decode, because it must be on if the Raw value is less than 371. Switch 1 requires checking to see if the Raw value is in the range between 460 and 371, where it is on by itself, or it can also be on with SW2, which makes the Raw value less than 275.

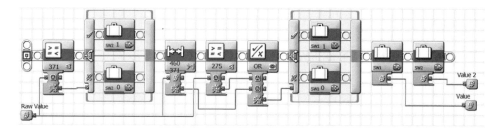

Figure 5-47. *Two switch decode My Block*

It's a good idea to run the test program in Figure 5-48 with your two switch input to make sure the values you're getting decode properly. The program displays the Raw value and the decoded state of the two switches. You might need to adjust the threshold levels to compensate for the particular resistor values you used.

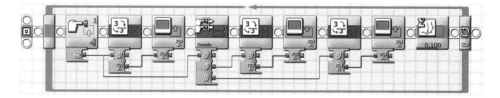

Figure 5-48. *Two switch test program*

CHAPTER 6

■■■

Potentiometer Sensors

A potentiometer, or pot for short, doesn't change in resistance with temperature like a thermistor, or light level like a CdS light-dependent resistor. It changes with the rotation of a mechanical shaft. You're probably already familiar with the device, because it's commonly used as the volume control on audio equipment. Rotating the shaft changes the resistance between the center and outer two terminals. It's a kind of self-contained voltage divider. Usually the shaft can only rotate 270 degrees, but multiturn versions are available. Figure 6-1 shows a few examples of potentiometers.

Figure 6-1. *A few examples of potentiometers*

Connecting to the Pot

A potentiometer is also a passive-type sensor, and is connected to the NXT using the same two connections you used for the contact and resistive sensors from Chapters 4 and 5. Connecting the NXT to the left and center terminals creates an angle sensor that increases in resistance with clockwise rotation, as shown in Figure 6-2. Connecting to the center and right terminals makes a counterclockwise sensor. In either case, it's a good idea to connect the remaining outer terminal to the center terminal.

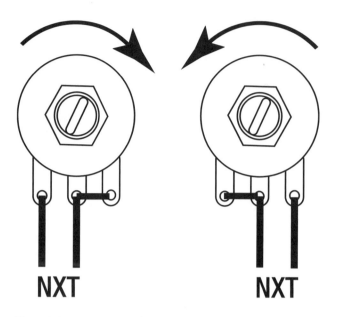

Figure 6-2. *Connections for clockwise and counterclockwise rotation*

Resistance Selection

Potentiometers come in many different full-scale resistance values and tapers. Linear taper means the resistance changes evenly with angle, and that's what you're looking for. You can write an equation for the resistance where A is the angle in degrees and R_{pot} is the full-scale resistance. Plugging that equation into the one you already have for Raw values leads to an equation that tells you what Raw value you'll get at any angle.

$$R = \frac{A}{270}\ R_{pot}\ [\Omega]$$

$$Raw = \frac{1023}{\left[\dfrac{2,700,000}{A\ R_{pot}}\right]+1}$$

Not surprisingly, the Raw value doesn't change linearly with angle. The plot in Figure 6-3 shows the results you'd get for three R_{pot} values. Clearly the Raw value for the 50kΩ changes the most in the first 90 degrees of rotation, but after that it levels off. In the range from 90 to 180 degrees, the 20kΩ pot changes the most of the three, and would be the best choice for applications with up to 180 degrees of rotation. For full 270-degree rotation, the 10kΩ is the best because in the 180-to-270 degree range it has the most change.

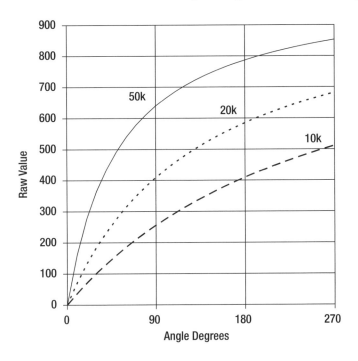

Figure 6-3. *Plot of Raw values versus shaft angle*

The pot resistance value you buy depends on how many degrees of rotation your application requires. The 10kΩ Raw values change almost linearly with angle, and if you were going to be marooned on a desert island, you'd pack the 10kΩ pot. However, picking the right resistance for your application greatly improves the angular resolution you'll get. The graph in Figure 6-4 shows the range of Raw values given that you're only using the pots in their optimal range. That is 90 degrees for the 50kΩ, 180 degrees for the 20kΩ, and 270 degrees for the 10kΩ.

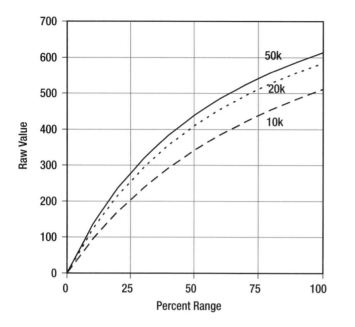

Figure 6-4. *Raw value over optimal operating range*

Angle Sensor Construction

The Bourns 3310C or 3310Y potentiometers make excellent angle sensors for the NXT. The 3310C in Figure 6-5 has three terminals on one side, while the 3310Y has them coming out the back in a triangle pattern. You should definitely solder your connections to these pots or the wires will pull off too easily.

Figure 6-5. *Bourns 3310C potentiometer*

Start by stripping the ends of the speaker wires about the same length as the terminals on the pot. Figure 6-6 shows all the components. Remember to have some heat shrink tubing slipped on the wires before you solder.

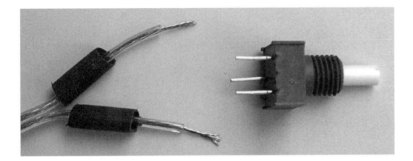

Figure 6-6. *Homebrew angle sensor step 1*

For the example in Figure 6-7, the angle sensor will increase in the counterclockwise direction. The connections might look backward, but remember the terminals are on the back of the 3310Y. Although it will work either way, it's a good idea to tie the unused outer terminal to the center. After the wire has been wrapped around the terminals, solder the connection.

Figure 6-7. *Homebrew angle sensor step 2*

Slide the heat shrink over the connection and shrink with a hair dryer. Your sensor should look like Figure 6-8.

Figure 6-8. *Homebrew angle sensor step 3*

The mounting hole size for the pot is 1/4 inch (6.355mm), which is just a little bigger in diameter than a Technic hole. Enlarging the hole is easy because you can drill through LEGO plastic with only a drill bit held in your fingers, or pliers, as shown in Figure 6-9.

Figure 6-9. *Hand drilling triangle beam*

A Technic triangle beam is an excellent part to modify because it's thin enough to use the mounting nut included with the potentiometer to fasten it. Figure 6-10 shows the pot mounted to the triangle beam. The NXT kit comes with two of these triangles, but you might want to buy some extras. A Technic Beams accessory kit is available from LEGO Shop at Home (PN#10072) that has a two triangles and a lot of other useful parts. I usually only drill out the center hole on the wide side of the triangle, and leave the rest of the holes for mounting to the project.

Figure 6-10. *Mounted angle sensor*

The shaft of the pot fits nicely in the 16- and 40-tooth gear centers with only friction. However, you can make a more universal connector by gluing a blue axle peg to the shaft. This needs to be done with a little fixture to ensure the proper alignment and positioning.

Build up the fixture shown in Figure 6-11 and make sure the little screwdriver slot in the end of the pot shaft is horizontal. Put a drop of gel-type fast-setting glue into the hollow of the axle peg. Slowly slide the triangle/pot assembly down so the pot shaft fits inside the peg. While you're pushing, watch that the glue is not pumping out and getting into the moving parts of the pot. Also make sure you fully seat the assembly against the spacers, as in Figure 6-12. Let the whole thing sit long enough for the glue to set fully.

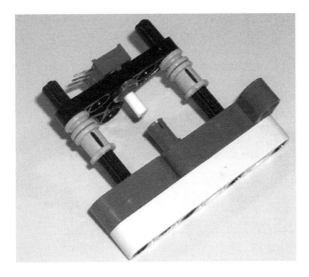

Figure 6-11. *Potentiometer blue axle peg mounting fixture*

Figure 6-12. *Fully seated*

NXT Protractor

Converting the measured Raw value into an angle only requires a little algebra. R_{pot} isn't a variable because it doesn't change once you pick the pot, so you can simplify the equation a little. This equation is coded in Figure 6-13 to make a NXT protractor that reads the pot angle and displays it on the screen.

$$A = \frac{2,700,000\ Raw}{R_{pot}(1023 - Raw)}\ \text{[degrees]}$$

$$A = \frac{G\ Raw}{1023 - Raw}\ \text{Where G = 54 for the 50k}\Omega\text{, 135 for the 20k}\Omega\text{, and 270 for the 10k}\Omega$$

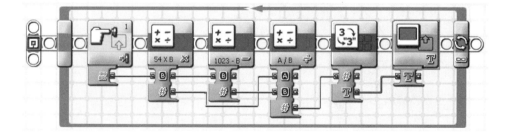

Figure 6-13. *NXT-G protractor program*

Pressure Sensor

Figure 6-14 shows how you can combine a potentiometer and a pneumatic cylinder to make a simple pressure sensor. The pneumatic cylinder tries to extend its piston when pressure is applied to the lower input, but two rubber bands resist the motion. The rubber bands exert a force that is linear with the amount they are stretched. That means the extent the pneumatic cylinder moves is directly related to the pressure in the cylinder. As the piston is pushed outward, it rotates a connecting arm connected to the pot. Because the total rotation is only about 90 degrees, use the 50kΩ pot.

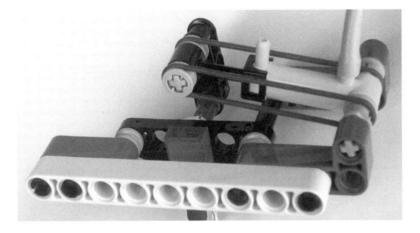

Figure 6-14. *Pressure sensor using pneumatic cylinder and 50kΩ pot*

LEGO rubber bands come in a variety of sizes and are color coded. Blue ones are large enough that they are barely stretched with the piston in the starting position. White ones are small enough that they are already stretched in the same position. You need to pick a color or combination of colors to set the range of pressures you want to measure. Figure 6-15 shows the pressure ranges we measured with two blue, one blue and one white, and two white rubber bands.

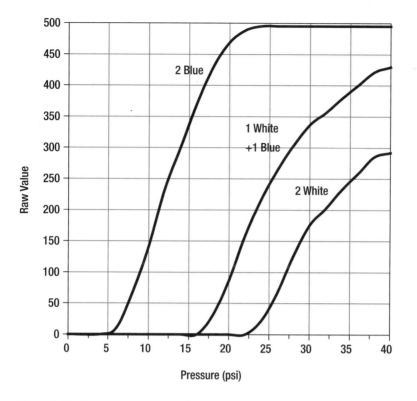

Figure 6-15. *Raw versus pressure for three different rubber band combinations*

Broom Balancer

You can probably balance a broom by the end of its handle on the open palm of your hand. It's not that hard because the broom's center of gravity is way up near the bristles, and it can't move as quickly as you can move the handle. Designing a machine that can balance a broom like this is not as easy as it might seem. People have earned PhDs in engineering studying this control problem. Although the example in Figure 6-16 works, it's just a starting point for further experimentation.

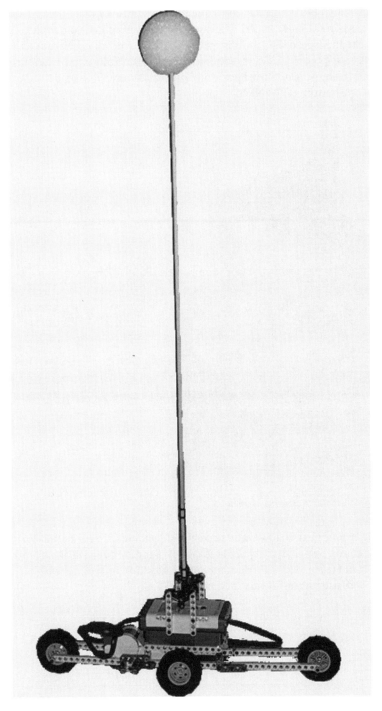

Figure 6-16. *Broom and balancer cart*

The 20kΩ pot is an excellent angle sensor for this application because it rotates with little friction, and only 180 degrees of motion is needed. The angle sensor is mounted so that the angle of the broom is directly measured. For simplicity, the Raw value is not converted to a true angle. You need to wire the pot for counterclockwise operation if it's mounted exactly as in Figure 6-17. You also need to adjust it so the 0Ω position is near the point where the broom is lying horizontally toward the bottom of the NXT.

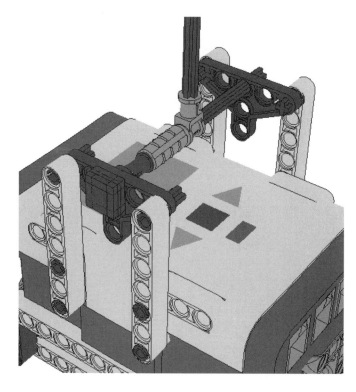

Figure 6-17. *Close-up of pivot mount for broom handle*

The NXT motors are internally geared down, and unfortunately their speed is a little slow for this application. You need the cart to move quickly to correct for the broom tilting even a little. The gear train shown in Figure 6-18 multiplies the motor speed by three. The two gear trains are in parallel to increase the torque-handling capability.

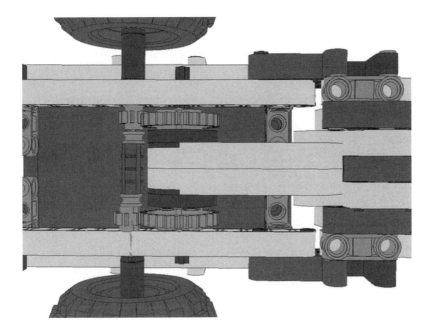

Figure 6-18. *Close-up of gear train for broom cart wheels*

The broom handle is made from a 3/16 inch (4.75mm) diameter, 25 inch (64cm) long wooden dowel rod. You can fasten it to the angle sensing axle in a variety of ways. Our favorite is to use two Technic socket joints, as shown in Figure 6-19. The dowel rod is pushed through the two holes on the sides of the joint sockets. A 2.5 inch (6.4cm) diameter Styrofoam ball tops the pole to make it act more like a broom.

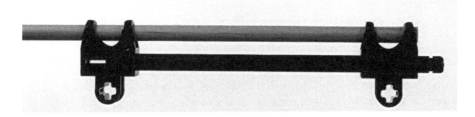

Figure 6-19. *Example broom handle holder*

The main program for the broom balancer is illustrated in Figure 6-20 and has two parts. The broom must be initially vertical and in the balanced position when the program is started. This position is remembered as X. Then the program goes into the endless loop of updating the control and driving the motor.

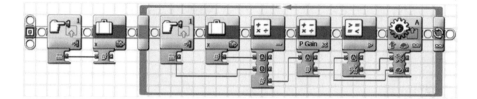

Figure 6-20. *Inverted pendulum main program*

The control loop reads the current pot value and subtracts the original value X from it. This creates an angle error, and the amount of power delivered to the motor is dependent on this error multiplied by a gain. The value of this gain depends on a lot of factors beyond the scope of this book, but you need to play with it to get good stability.

Joysticks

Joysticks are great for manual and remote-control applications. You can combine two angle sensors in a simple gimbal mount to make a joystick. This is a good application for the 50kΩ pot because its total angle of motion is only about 90 degrees.

Bottom Mounted Joystick

You can build a remote-control platform with the joystick on the bottom of the NXT, as shown in Figure 6-21. Building it on the bottom leaves the display and control buttons free for other things. For example, you can operate the joystick with one hand and push the buttons with the other.

The test program in Figure 6-22 allows you to check the operation of your joystick. You need to hold the NXT so you can see the display, but you're moving the joystick from behind. Moving the handle left and right should move the Aim image shown in Figure 6-23 back and forth on the display. Moving the handle up and down moves the image top to bottom on the display.

Figure 6-21. *Joystick built on the bottom of the NXT*

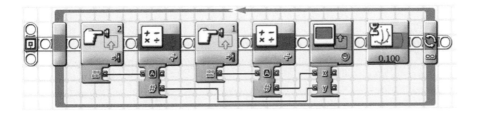

Figure 6-22. *Joystick test program*

Figure 6-23. *Joystick test display*

Top Mounted Joystick for the T-56

The T-56 Robot Arm project included with the NXT is limited to preprogrammed movements. Adding a joystick control (see Figure 6-24) lets you swing and elevate the arm to any position you want. You can also program the left and right NXT buttons to open and close the jaw on command.

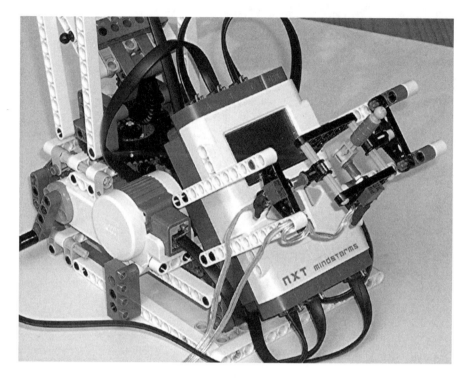

Figure 6-24. *Front mounted joystick for the T-56 robot arm*

The joystick gimbal for the front mount is the same as the back mount joystick. If it's mounted far enough above the NXT, the display and buttons are still accessible. Because the T-56 already makes use of input ports 1 and 3, the swing axis control has to be brought into port 2 and the elevation axis into port 4.

The idle position of the joystick is recorded when the program first starts. These raw values are saved in variables C0 and B0, as shown in Figure 6-25. Then the program goes into a long endless loop of moving the two axes and checking if the jaw should open or close.

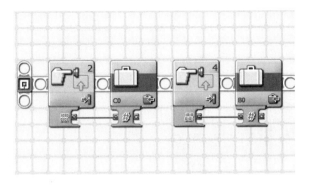

Figure 6-25. *T-56 program initialization*

The control is exactly the same for both axes, as seen in Figures 6-26 and 27. The current value of the pot is read and subtracted from the initial position to create a motor power command. The direction of the command is determined by comparing the value to zero. Fortunately, the Motor block doesn't care if the power command is positive or negative; it just uses the size of the number.

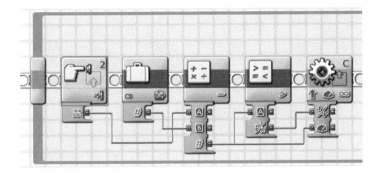

Figure 6-26. *First axis control*

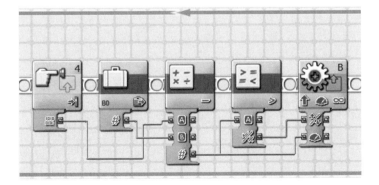

Figure 6-27. *Second axis control*

The jaw control part of the NXT-G program checks if the left or right NXT button has been pressed, as shown in Figure 6-28. A fixed 0.5s command is issued to the jaw motor that opens or closes it.

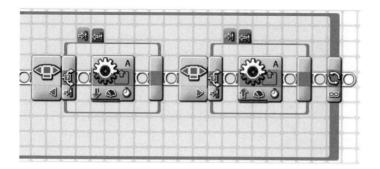

Figure 6-28. *Jaw control*

CHAPTER 7

■ ■ ■

Voltage Sensors

In Chapter 5 you learned that the NXT converts the voltage on a sensor input into a digital value. Until now, the only voltage being converted was the 5V supply inside the NXT, or some part of it divided through an external resistor. It probably doesn't come as a big surprise that you can connect an external voltage to the input and have the NXT convert that instead.

■**Caution** *Never* connect these voltage sensors to anything but low voltage battery-operated equipment. Connecting them to household electricity could be lethal both to you and the NXT.

Design of a –5V to +5V Sensor

Figure 7-1 shows a circuit diagram of the NXT input with a simple voltage sensor. The only component needed is a 10kΩ resistor. The external voltage you're going to measure is labeled as E on the circuit. Some examples should help you to understand how it works.

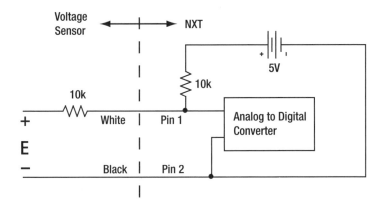

Figure 7-1. *–5V to +5V sensor circuit*

First, suppose the external voltage E is 0V. That's the same as connecting the external 10kΩ resistor across the input, like you've been doing for the last three chapters. The NXT's 5V is going to be evenly divided between two 10kΩ resistors. That means the voltage at the analog-to-digital converter will be 2.5V, and that will be converted to a Raw value of about 512. This is the center point on Figure 7-2.

Next, suppose the external voltage E is 5V. Now the input is being pulled up to 5V through 10kΩ resistors both internally and externally. The input doesn't have any choice but to be 5V, which will be converted to a Raw value of 1,023. That is the top right point on Figure 7-2.

Finally, suppose the external voltage is –5V. The internal 10kΩ resistor is pulling the input up to 5V, and the external 10kΩ resistor is pulling the input down to –5V. That evenly matched tug-of-war results in 0V, which converts to a Raw value of 0, and which is plotted as the lower left point on Figure 7-2.

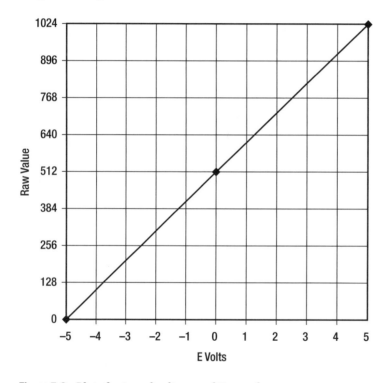

Figure 7-2. *Plot of external voltage and Raw value*

The following equation calculates the external voltage E knowing the measured Raw value:

$$E = \left[\frac{2}{1023} \frac{Raw}{} - 1 \right] 5 \; [\text{V}]$$

The integer arithmetic of the NXT would really cause a problem if you blindly tried to code this equation into a program. Without a decimal point, the result of the first division would only result in 0, 1, or 2, which would be a very coarse measurement of voltage. The way around this problem is to scale up the numbers by 1,000 and make sure you always multiply before you divide. After multiplying by 1,000 you end up with a smaller unit of voltage known as a millivolt, or mV:

$$E = \frac{10,000 \; Raw}{1023} - 5,000 \; \text{[mV]}$$

The program in Figure 7-3 reads the input and passes the Raw value through the parts of the equation. The voltage, scaled by 1,000, is then displayed on the screen. You could add some additional blocks to display a decimal point, but that detail is left to you. If nothing is connected to the input, the display will read 5000, which is just the 5V supply internal to the NXT.

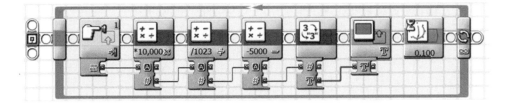

Figure 7-3. *NXT –5V to +5V voltmeter program*

Constructing the Voltage Sensor

Unlike the sensors in the previous chapters, you need to pay attention to which wire is connected to the black and which to the white. If you look carefully, one of the two 18 gauge (0.8mm²) speaker wires will have some kind of identification. For example, some speaker wire has a stripe painted on one side. Make the identified wire the one you connect to the black cable wire and it will become the – terminal of your voltage sensor. Naturally, the other wire will become the + terminal.

The best place to put the 10kΩ resistor is at the junction between the NXT cable and the speaker wire. You can attach it using a terminal block, but soldering is more compact and permanent. Cut the speaker wire so that the wire to be connected to the black cable wire is about 1/4 inch (10mm) longer to compensate for the length of the resistor. It makes the assembly look much neater. Figure 7-4 shows all the parts except the heat shrink.

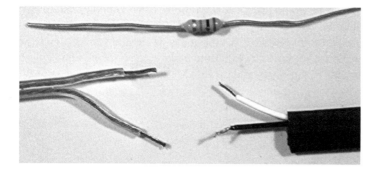

Figure 7-4. *Voltage sensor step 1*

Put a short piece of heat shrink tubing on the longer speaker wire and solder it to the black wire in the NXT cable. Slide the heat shrink down to cover the connection and shrink it with a hair dryer. Then solder the 10kΩ resistor (brown-black-orange-gold) to the white wire in the cable. Shrink some tubing over the end of the resistor and the connection. It should now look like Figure 7-5.

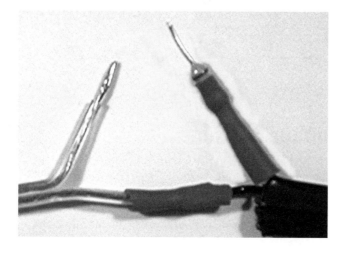

Figure 7-5. *Voltage sensor step 2*

Slip some heat shrink tubing over the resistor and solder the remaining connection. Then pull the tubing back over the resistor and shrink it so it looks like Figure 7-6.

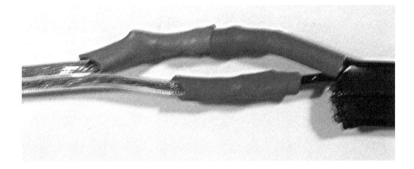

Figure 7-6. *Voltage sensor step 3*

Finally, shrink a large piece of tubing over the whole assembly, including a short length of the NXT cable. This provides strain relief and further protects the connections. The finished voltage sensor should look like Figure 7-7.

Figure 7-7. *Voltage sensor step 4*

NXT Battery Tester

Probably the most useful voltage to measure with the NXT voltmeter is an AA battery. It's always a good idea to check to see if there is any life left before throwing batteries away. You can make the AA holder from just a few LEGO parts, as shown in Figure 7-8. Electrical connection is made by stripping about an inch (25mm) of insulation off the ends of the speaker wire and looping it through the holes at the end of the beams. The + wire should go to the rotating beam on the top and the – wire to the one on the bottom. Wrapping aluminum foil around the end of the beams makes getting a good connection easier.

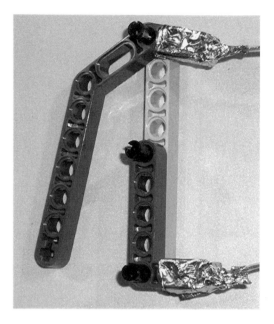

Figure 7-8. *Partial assembly of AA holder*

The AA battery is pinched much like a nut in a nutcracker between the ends of the beams, as shown in Figure 7-9. You should read the voltage using the NXT voltmeter program first to make sure everything works. If your meter reads a negative voltage, you mixed up the wires somehow and you need to exchange them.

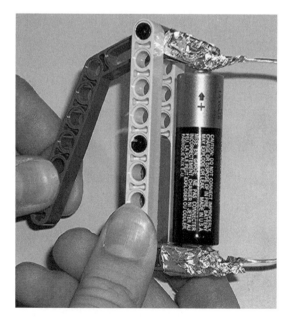

Figure 7-9. *Using the AA holder to measure battery voltage*

A simple battery tester program is shown in Figure 7-10. It classifies the battery quality into three bands. Above 1.45V, the battery is considered "Fantastic," between 1.45V and 1.25V it's "Good," and below 1.25V the battery is "Low."

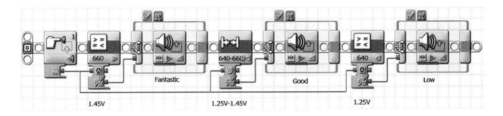

Figure 7-10. *Battery tester program*

A −15V to +15V Sensor

Five volts isn't always a wide enough measurement range. Laboratory instruments have an output signal for connecting to other instruments that's in the range of 0V to +10V. Industrial sensors are often −10V to +10V. Automotive electronics are around 12V, and 9V is common in portable electronics such as the NXT itself.

The voltage sensor design in Figure 7-11 allows the input signal to swing from -15V to +15V, and it only needs two resistors. You can get 15kΩ (5% color code: brown-green-orange-gold) resistors from Radio Shack in their assortment packs, but if you don't want to buy the 30kΩ (5% color code: orange-black-orange-gold) from another supplier, you need to make it from two 15kΩ resistors in series.

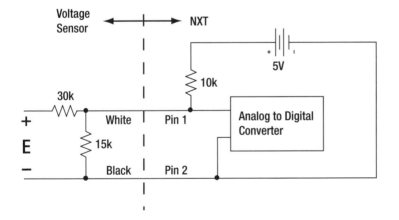

Figure 7-11. *−15V to +15V sensor circuit*

Figure 7-12 shows the plot of external voltage and Raw value. The program in Figure 7-13 is basically the same as the –5V to +5V program, only the numbers are scaled up by a factor of three.

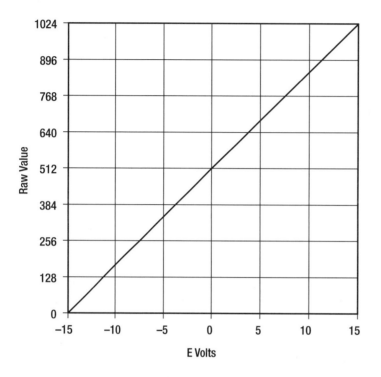

Figure 7-12. *Plot of input voltage and Raw value*

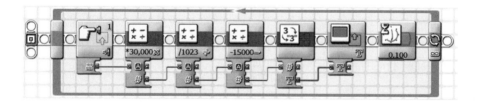

Figure 7-13. *–15V to +15V NXT voltmeter program*

CHAPTER 8

■ ■ ■

4.3V Powered Sensors

The NXT provides a DC voltage on the sensor input port for sensors that require a power supply. The LEGO Light and Sound Sensors are examples of sensors powered this way. It's defined as the 4.3V power supply, but the voltage actually varies about 7% with load. The plot in Figure 3-2 shows the voltage ranging from 4.6V, when is the power supply is lightly loaded, to 4.0V when it's fully loaded.

Hall Effect Sensor

The Hall Effect describes a magnetic field phenomenon in semiconducting materials. Without getting overly technical, electrons moving in a semiconductor are deflected by a magnetic field. The amount of deflection depends on the strength and orientation of the field. The deflection becomes a voltage that can be processed and converted into a switch-like output. Panasonic makes the DN6849 switch-type Hall Effect sensor (Digi-Key #DN6849SE-ND). The DN6848 is a similar but discontinued part.

Figure 8-1 shows the internal block diagram of the DN6849SE. The voltage generated by the Hall element is very small and requires an amplifier. Following the amplifier is a block of circuitry called a Schmitt trigger. It decides if the level is above a threshold and turns the switch on. It also prevents the output from rapidly toggling on and off when the level is equal to the threshold. Finally, the output is a transistor that's well-matched to the NXT sensor input.

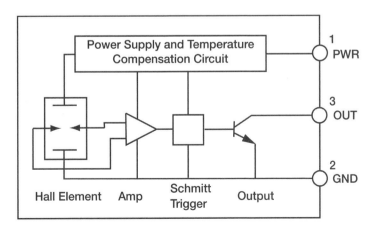

Figure 8-1. *DN6849SE Hall Effect sensor block diagram*

Hall Sensor Construction

The DN6849SE is so simple it can be connected directly to the end of a cut NXT cable, and it's so small it can be used without extensive packaging. The outline and pin out of the device is shown in Figure 8-2.

PWR GND OUT

Figure 8-2. *DN6849SE pin out*

The green wire in the NXT cable connects to the left, the black to the center, and the white to the right leg of the part. Figures 8-3 and 8-4 show the construction steps. Use heat shrink tubing to protect and insulate the connections.

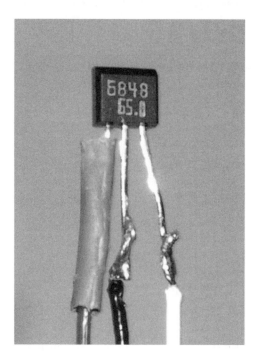

Figure 8-3. *Hall Sensor construction step 1*

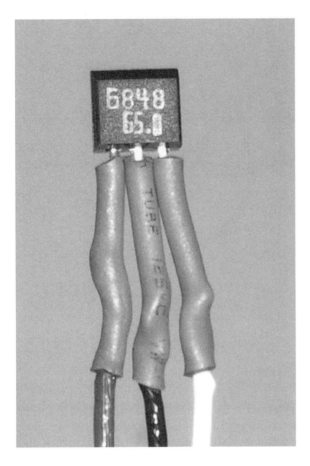

Figure 8-4. *Hall Sensor construction step 2*

Robot Mouse

Scientific research has proven that mice actually don't like cheese! However, the myth that mice love the smelly stuff will probably never die. This robot mouse has a Hall Effect sensor for a nose and thinks a magnet is its cheese.

The NXT Quick Start Vehicle is an excellent starting point for the robot mouse. All you need to add is a little boom to hold the Hall Sensor out in front, as shown in Figure 8-5. The height is adjusted so that the sensor just passes over the magnet without touching it. In this case, the magnet is a LEGO train car coupler, but it could be any small permanent magnet.

Figure 8-5. *NXT robot mouse with Hall Effect nose*

The NXT-G mouse program shown in Figure 8-6 has two parallel branches. The top branch simply keeps sweeping the robot back and forth with a slow forward motion. The bottom branch waits for the Hall Sensor to "smell" something, then it brakes the motors and stops the program. You could add some sniffing sounds and maybe a final yummy sound at the end.

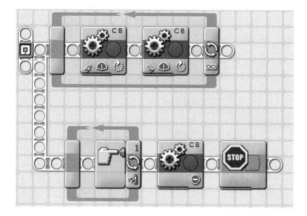

Figure 8-6. *NXT-G robot mouse program*

Transistor Buffer

Not every sensor you want to hook up to the NXT can connect as easily as the DN6849SE.
Either the 10kΩ resistor inside the NXT is too much load, or the 5V supply causes trouble.
A transistor buffer shown in Figure 8-7 is the perfect solution to the problem. The transistor
does the dirty work of driving the NXT input and isolating the 5 volt supply from the sensor.
This design is not foolproof; if you plug it into a motor port it will most likely be damaged. In
the section "Enhancing the Transistor Buffer" we'll suggest an enhancement that fixes that.

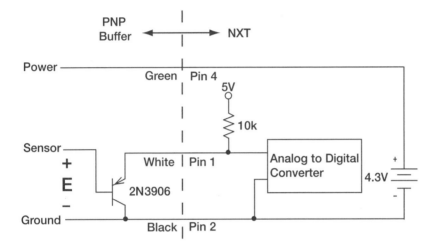

Figure 8-7. *Transistor buffer with NXT sensor input circuitry*

The transistor in the circuit is a PNP type, and the symbol for it is shown in Figure 8-8
along with its pin out. The transistor doesn't need much gain, only faces low voltages, and
handles practically no current. Probably the most common small-signal PNP transistor such
as this in a leaded package is the 2N3906. Radio Shack sells them in packages of 15.

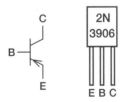

Figure 8-8. *PNP transistor symbol and 2N3906 pin out*

This one transistor circuit is called a voltage follower because the voltage on the transistor emitter just follows the voltage on the base without any gain. In fact, the emitter voltage does follow the base, but with an offset voltage of about 0.6V, as you can see in Figure 8-9.

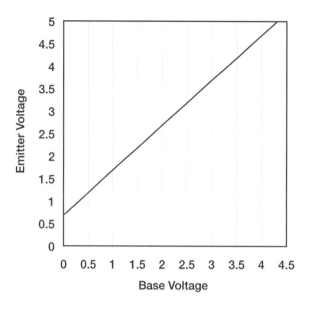

Figure 8-9. *Follower base and emitter voltages*

The emitter voltage is the same as the input to the NXT analog-to-digital converter, so you can easily figure out the Raw value. However, if the NXT thinks it has a LEGO Light Sensor connected, it scales the Raw value into a range from 0 to 100 (see Figure 8-10), otherwise known as the Percent scale. It isn't really the mathematical percent of anything; it just looks like a percent. This equation defines the conversion where P is limited to the range 0 to 100:

$$P = 127 - int(\frac{Raw}{7})$$

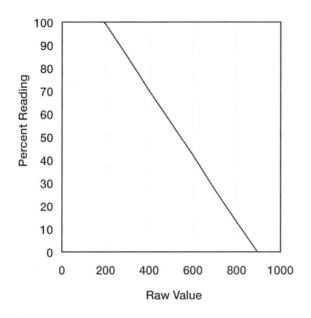

Figure 8-10. *Raw value versus light value*

We can combine all this knowledge to produce a graph of percent reading and the voltage on the transistor base (see Figure 8-11). With a little bit of fringe on the ends, the 0 to 100 range nicely maps the voltage range you're likely to get from a sensor powered from 4.3V.

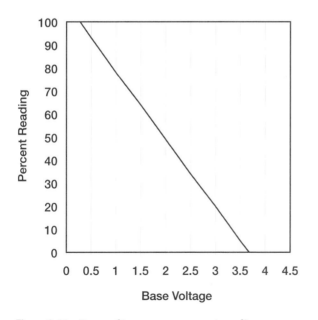

Figure 8-11. *Base voltage versus percent reading*

Construction of the buffer (see Figure 8-12) only requires connecting the transistor to the end of a cut NXT cable, much like the Hall Sensor. Power for the sensor is available on the green wire. The black wire is connected to the collector of the transistor and is the ground for the sensor. The base terminal of the transistor is where the sensor signal is connected, and the white wire is only connected to the emitter of the transistor.

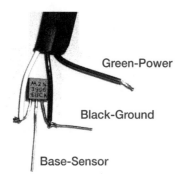

Figure 8-12. *PNP transistor buffer construction*

Infrared Rangefinder

Figure 8-13 is a photograph of the Sharp GP2D12 (Acroname #R48-IR12), which is a self-contained infrared rangefinder. It measures distances from 4 inches (10cm) to 31 inches (80cm). Infrared rangefinders are typically used in equipment such as copy machines to measure the location of paper or other moving parts. One advantage of the GP2D12 over the NXT Ultrasonic Distance Sensor is that it's unaffected by other distance sensors that might be operating nearby.

Figure 8-13. *GP2D12 infrared rangefinder*

It works by sending out a short burst of infrared light from an LED every 32ms. The beam is dark red and barely visible to the naked eye. If you look at it with a digital camera, you can clearly see the beam, as in Figure 8-14. The beam is fairly narrow and is only about 2 inches (6cm) in diameter at a distance of 31 inches (80cm).

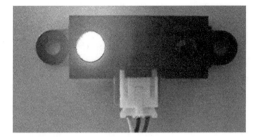

Figure 8-14. *Infrared beam as seen with a digital camera*

The block diagram of the sensor is shown in Figure 8-15. A type of one-dimensional camera called a Position Sensing Device (PSD) is then used to receive the reflection of the beam from an object in front of the sensor. The distance to the object is directly related to where along the one-dimensional image the spot lies. The sensor outputs a voltage between 0.4V and 2.4V, and is roughly inversely proportional to the distance. That is, the farther away the object, the lower the output voltage.

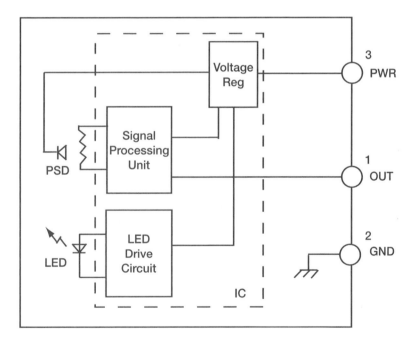

Figure 8-15. *GP2D12 block diagram*

Unfortunately, the GP2D12 cannot be connected directly to the NXT sensor input. The sensor should not have the output pin pulled above the power supply, but the 10kΩ pull up resistor inside the NXT tries to do just that. The GP2D12 also doesn't have enough output power to handle the load of the 10kΩ resistor. Fortunately, the transistor buffer is here to save the day.

Interface Construction

The GP2D12 has a tiny connector known as a JST. Make sure you order the matching prewired connector when you order the sensor. Although it's possible to solder directly to the connector, we wouldn't recommend it. The three pins in the connector are laid out as shown in Figure 8-16, but you probably only need to use this if the prewired connector you buy is not color coded. Otherwise, use Table 8-1 and Figure 8-17 to build the interface.

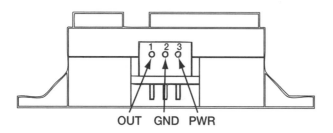

Figure 8-16. *GP2D12 outline and pin out*

Table 8-1. *Connections for the GP2D12*

Pin	Function	GP2D12 Wire Color	NXT Cable Color
1	Output	Yellow	Transistor Base
2	Ground	Black	Black
3	Power	Red	Green

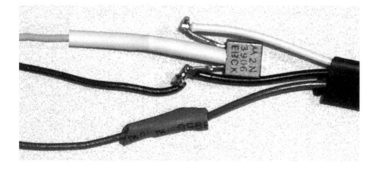

Figure 8-17. *Transistor buffer for the GP2D12 interface*

Operation of the Sensor

When you use the infrared rangefinder, configure the sensor input port to be an NXT Light Sensor. The reading will be in the Percent scale, and the value will range from 30 for a distance of about 4 inches (10cm) to 100 for a distance of 31 inches (80cm). As you can see in the plot in Figure 8-18, the value is not linear with distance. Nobody seems to know why, but at distances shorter than 4 inches (10cm), the relationship actually reverses and the Percent values increase.

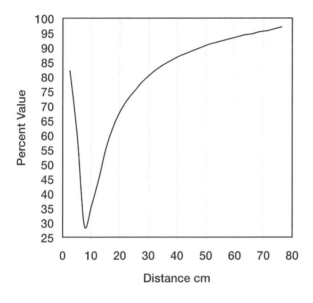

Figure 8-18. *Plot of distance and Percent value*

■**Note** The pulsing of the LED creates a lot of electrical noise in the NXT. You can't hear it, but the LEGO Sound Sensor picks it up through its power supply connection. The Sound Sensor picks up so much noise this way, it's essentially useless. There doesn't seem to be any practical way to allow the two sensors to coexist when connected to the same NXT.

Wall Follower

Wall following is a basic function for maze-running robots. The NXT Quick Start robot is the ideal platform, and the infrared rangefinder is the ideal sensor for the task. The mounting holes on the GP2D12 are the wrong size and spacing to mount directly to Technic beams. However, you can arrange four Technic double-axle rubber joiners as in Figure 8-19 to give the right amount of compliance to hold the sensor tightly to the side of a bent lift arm beam. The GP2D12's mounting ears slip perfectly between the beam and the axles. The sensor is tilted back so it looks ahead of the robot.

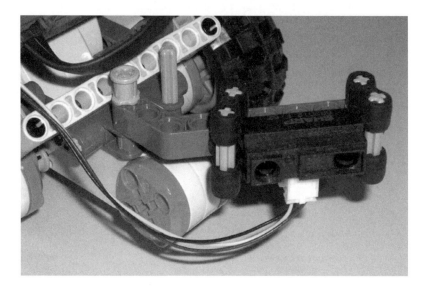

Figure 8-19. *Wall follower*

The NXT-G program is shown in Figure 8-20. A Move block makes programming the wall follower easy because it has a single steering command that simultaneously controls two motors. It turns by an amount proportional to the steering command, with zero going straight. The desired distance to the wall, in this case 90, is subtracted from the distance reading, and this becomes the steering command value. The value of the sensor is also displayed for debugging.

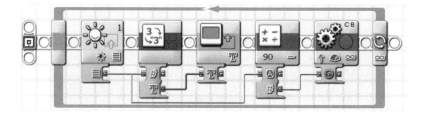

Figure 8-20. *NXT-G wall follower program*

Differential Light Sensor

Occasionally the measurement you really need is the difference between two levels, and not the levels themselves. Measuring the two levels and calculating the difference in software not only uses two input ports, but can also limit the accuracy of the result. For example, suppose you just want to know the difference in the amount of light in two places. The overall range of light levels could be huge, but the range of conversion is limited. The difference between a light reading of 85 and 90 is a big difference in light level, but would only be numerically 5. One way around this problem is to design a sensor that subtracts the difference before the conversion.

We covered the characteristics of the Cadmium Sulfide LDR in Chapter 5. These are resistors that change in value with light level. If you put a voltage across two identical LDRs in series as in Figure 8-21, then the center connection will be exactly half of the voltage. As long as the amount of light is the same, the voltage will always be half. If one sensor receives less light, then its resistance will increase, and the center voltage will move proportionally.

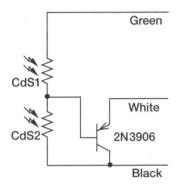

Figure 8-21. *Differential Light Sensor circuit diagram*

It would be nice just to hook this center point up to the sensor input of the NXT, but there would be a problem. The 10kΩ pull-up resistor inside the NXT would throw everything off. In low light conditions, the LDRs would each have a resistance of around 100kΩ. Being ten times smaller, the 10kΩ would dominate the resistance, and you would mostly measure it and not the LDRs. So, you need to use a transistor buffer again.

Construction

The two CdS sensors are constructed just like those in Chapter 5. You need to connect them in series, tying the center point to the base of the transistor buffer. The CdS sensors in Figure 8-22 are outside the borders of the photo to the left. Tie one of the two ends to the power supply (green) wire and the other to the ground (black) wire. You can use heat shrink to protect and insulate the connections. Figures 8-23 and 24 take you step by step through the rest of the process.

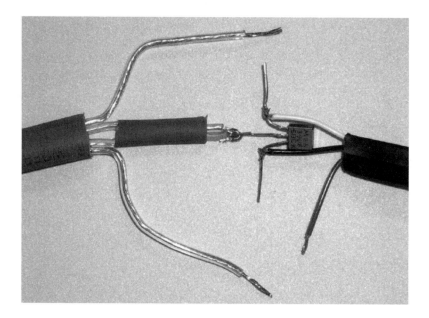

Figure 8-22. *Center point of CdS sensors tied to the transistor base*

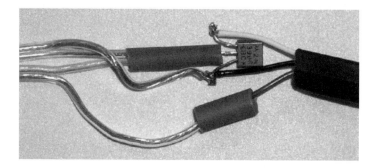

Figure 8-23. *Connect the 4.3V power to a remaining wire and the ground to the other.*

Figure 8-24. *Heat shrink tubing goes over the entire assembly.*

Digital Sundial

Sundials are one of the world's oldest inventions. Most of them are just an object to block the sun, called the *gnomon*, and a dial with time values printed on it. They work by casting a shadow of the gnomon onto the dial. You can use the differential Light Sensor to make a sundial that tries not to cast a shadow by keeping its gnomon pointed directly at the sun.

The gnomon sits between the two Light Sensors, as seen in Figure 8-25. The whole assembly is mounted directly on an NXT motor shaft so it can rotate to track the sun. Over the course of a day, the sun travels across the sky in an arc from east to west. The plane of the arc is at an angle that changes throughout the year. It will be low in the sky in the winter and practically overhead in the summer. The tracking motor is on an adjustable mount, seen in Figure 8-26, that can be tilted to point at the sun. You should point the NXT due south before starting the program.

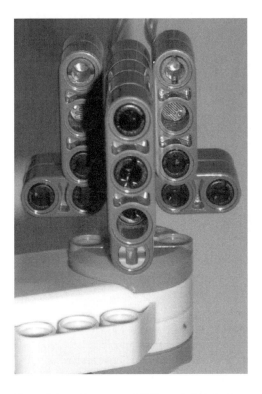

Figure 8-25. *Close-up of differential Light Sensor and gnomon*

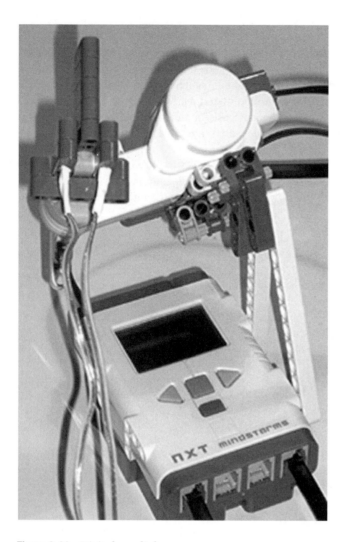

Figure 8-26. *Digital sundial*

The sundial program tries to keep the value of the differential Light Sensor near the balanced light position by turning the motor. You might think that the balanced value would be 50 because that's in the middle of the 0-to-100 range, but it isn't. If the supply voltage is 4.6V, then half the supply voltage would be 2.3V. Looking up 2.3V on Figure 8-11 says the balance point is around 45. Allowing a small amount of imbalance prevents the motor from constantly tracking back and forth around the point. It only moves when the value is less than 40 or greater than 50.

The first thing the program does is swing the gnomon around till a beam contacts a touch switch at the six o'clock position (see Figure 8-27). This establishes the angular zero point. Then the program goes into an endless loop that orients the gnomon and displays the time (see Figure 8-28). Depending on which side of the gnomon your CdS Light Sensors are mounted, you might need to reverse both of the Motor block directions. If you have them backward, the sundial will actually try to avoid the sun.

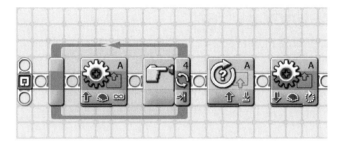

Figure 8-27. *Sundial program initialization*

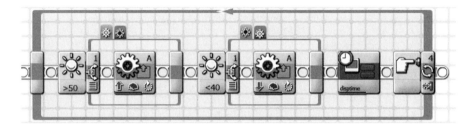

Figure 8-28. *Sundial program main loop*

You compute the time by converting the motor angle into hours and minutes (see Figure 8-29). The My Block conversion isn't fancy. It doesn't do a.m. and p.m. or daylight savings time, and when the minute is less than 10, it doesn't even add the customary leading zero. The time display does add a colon between the hours and minutes, as shown in Figure 8-30.

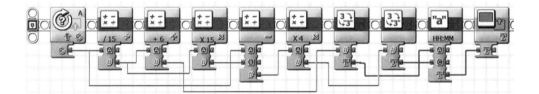

Figure 8-29. *Angle to time display My Block*

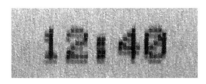

Figure 8-30. *Sundial time display*

Enhancing the Transistor Buffer

The NXT only has one type of cable for both motors and sensors. That means you can plug a sensor into a motor port. As you might expect, LEGO has gone to great lengths to make sure this won't damage its sensors. However, the transistor buffer isn't so forgiving. If you want to make your transistor buffers more foolproof, the addition of a 470Ω resistor between the emitter and white wire will protect the transistor should the sensor be accidentally plugged into the wrong place.

CHAPTER 9

■ ■ ■

Two-Wire Powered Sensors

The original LEGO MINDSTORMS brick, the RCX, used a two-wire powered sensor interface. The NXT has a backward compatibility mode with the old RCX sensors, and that mode offers some advantages for homebrew sensors that need higher voltages than the 4.3V supply described in Chapter 8. It's a natural choice for sensors that need to take full advantage of the 5V analog-to-digital conversion. Conveniently, the two wires are the same two wires you already used for passive sensors: the white and black wires in the NXT cable, or pins 1 and 2 on the port connector.

Signals

Power and sensor readings are combined on two wires by splitting the functions in time. First the sensor signal is read, with exactly the same method as the passive sensors described in Chapters 4 through 7, except the signal is only read during a short 0.1ms window of time. After that, power is applied to the two wires for about 3ms. Figure 9-1 graphically shows the timing, but the passive time interval is much shorter than the power. The NXT keeps cycling between these two intervals as long as the port is configured as a two-wire powered sensor.

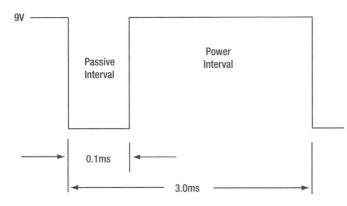

Figure 9-1. *Timing for the two-wire powered sensor (not drawn to scale)*

Figure 9-2 shows the minimal two-wire powered sensor. Diode D1 separates the power part of the cycle from the passive. Diodes act like one-way valves for current, and oriented in the direction shown, D1 will only conduct when the NXT voltage is greater than the voltage on C1. The diode symbol looks like an arrow pointing at a line, and the line end of the part is called the cathode. The real part has a line painted on the cathode end too. The other end is called the anode. With new batteries, the voltage on C1 approaches 9V, but with weak ones it might only be 6V. Either way, it will always be greater than the 5V used by the NXT to read the sensor.

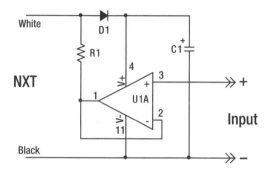

Figure 9-2. *Minimal two-wire powered sensor*

The large triangle symbol in the circuit is an operational amplifier, or op-amp for short. There are many kinds of op-amp, but the pin numbers in the figure correspond to the LM324. Actually, the LM324 contains four op-amps like this in the same 14 pin package. Explaining exactly how an op-amp works is beyond the scope of this book, but basically it's an amplifier whose output is on the corner of the triangle on the left. The NXT reads whatever voltage the op-amp output has through resistor R1.

Remember that the NXT has a 10kΩ resistor pulling the white wire up to 5V. If the op-amp output is 0V, then the voltage the NXT reads will be the result of a voltage divider R1, which is 1kΩ, and the internal 10kΩ resistor to 5V. That results in 0.45V or a Raw value of 93. If the op-amp output is 5V, the NXT input voltage will also be 5V, which results in a Raw value of 1,023. So, at best, this sensor creates Raw values between 93 and 1,023. Op-amps such as the LM324 can only bring their outputs down to about 0.65V, so the low end of the range is actually limited to something like 214. General instructions for building this type of sensor are given in Appendix A.

Programming

Several programming languages are available for the NXT. The easiest to understand is the programming language that comes with the NXT, known as NXT-G. Next Byte Codes (NBC) is a more complicated language, but because we're getting to more complicated sensors, it's worth looking at programs written in that language too. You can obtain complete listings of the programs from the book website (go to the Source Code/Download area at www.apress.com) and from Appendix B of the book.

NXT-G

NXT-G has a block for the RCX-style Light Sensor called the Light* block. You can use it for all two-wire powered sensors (see Figure 9-3). There's an output from the block with the usual 0–100 light value, but we're more interested in the Raw value. It should be easy to figure out how to convert the NBC programs in this chapter into NXT-G programs by using the Light* block.

—Raw

Figure 9-3. *NXT-G Light* block*

NBC

NBC is not graphical and not as easy to use as NXT-G, but it offers some advantages for writing complex programs. It requires some tedious declarations (partially shown in Listing 9-1) that include which sensor port you're using, what type of sensor you connected there, and what type of result you want.

Listing 9-1. *NBC Sensor Declarations*

```
thePort byte IN_1 // sensor port 1
theSensorType byte IN_TYPE_REFLECTION  //RCX style light
theSensorMode byte IN_MODE_RAW // raw data mode
```

Internally, the NXT is doing several things at once. The sensors are managed by a different process than the one that runs your program. You have to set up port configuration values and trigger the sensor management process to reset the sensor to the new values. These programming steps are given in Listing 9-2. Reading the value is the single line of code given in Listing 9-3, where RVal contains the current sensor Raw value.

Listing 9-2. *NBC Sensor Reset Sequence*

```
setin   theSensorType, thePort, Type    // write sensor type to port
setin   theSensorMode, thePort, InputMode // write sensor mode to port
set     isInvalid, TRUE  // invalidate the sensor
setin   isInvalid, thePort, InvalidData
```

```
stillInvalid:          // loop until it is not invalid
   getin  isInvalid, thePort, InvalidData
   brtst  NEQ, stillInvalid, isInvalid
setin  SVal, thePort, ScaledValue   // reset the scaled value
```

Listing 9-3. *NBC Read Sensor*

```
getin  RVal, thePort, RawValue  // read in new value
```

Half-Volt Sensor

Figure 9-4 shows the circuit for a voltage sensor that reads input voltages between –0.5V and +0.5V. Diode D2 has been added to the basic Figure 9-2 design to provide an offset voltage. When diodes conduct, they behave a little like a 0.58V battery. The positive input on the op-amp in this circuit with the components listed in Table 9-1 will have a gain of 1+R1/R2, 1+330/100, or 4.3. With no voltage on the negative input, the output of the op-amp will be offset by 0.58×4.3 or 2.49V. This offset will allow you to measure negative voltages.

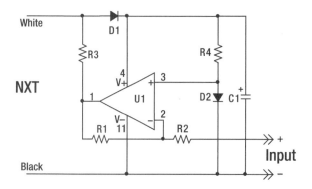

Figure 9-4. *Half-volt sensor circuit*

Table 9-1. *Bill of Materials*

Component	Part Number	Description	Radio Shack
U1	LM324	Quad OpAmp	276-1711
D1, D2	1N4148	Small Signal Diodes	276-1122
R1	330kΩ	1/4 W 5% Carbon Film Resistor (orange-orange-yellow-gold) For All Resistors	271-312
R3	1kΩ	1/4 W 5% Carbon Film Resistor (brown-black-red-gold)	See R1
R2	100kΩ	1/4 W 5% Carbon Film Resistor (brown-black-brown-gold)	See R1
R4	10kΩ	1/4 W 5% Carbon Film Resistor (brown-black-yellow-gold)	See R1
C1	22uF	16V or Higher Electrolytic Capacitor	272-1014

The gain of the negative input is R1/R2 or 3.3. The negative input inverts the voltage so a positive input subtracts from the output voltage. For example, with an input of +0.5V, the op-amp output will be the offset 2.49V minus 1.65V, which equals 0.84V. Notice that the more positive the input voltage, the smaller the op-amp output voltage, the smaller the NXT input voltage, and the smaller the Raw value.

The usable range of the voltage sensor is limited by the low voltage capability of the op-amp and how weak the NXT batteries are. It should give good results between −0.5V and +0.5V, with the relationship of input voltage to Raw value shown in Figure 9-5. After all the circuit gains and offsets, the 0V input is offset by about 560, and the slope is 1.6mV per Raw value.

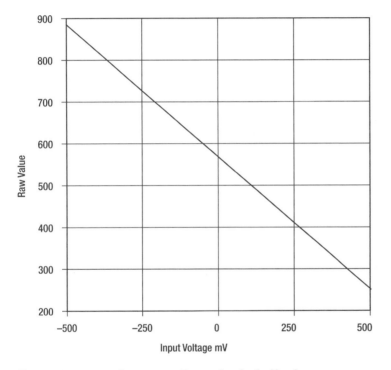

Figure 9-5. *Input voltage versus Raw value for half-volt sensor*

Construction of the sensor follows the same techniques described in Appendix A. Figure 9-6 shows the circuit built on a solderless breadboard, Table 9-2 has the step-by-step instructions for connecting the parts, and Figure 9-7 shows the sensor moved to a PC board.

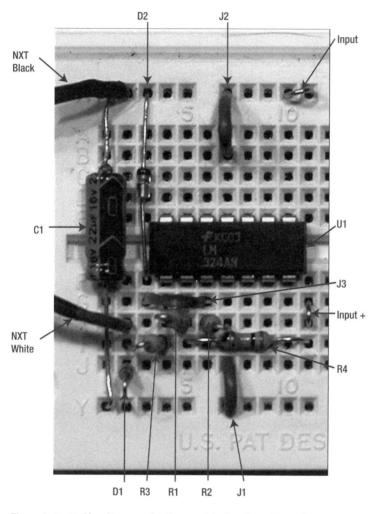

Figure 9-6. *Half-volt sensor built on solderless breadboard*

Table 9-2. *Component Placement*

Component	Start	End
U1 pin 1	F4	
C1 + –	Y1	X1
J1	Y7	J7
J2	X7	B7
D1 anode cathode (the cathode is the end with the line)	J2	Y2
D2 anode cathode	F3	X3
J3	G6	G3
R3 (brown-black-red-gold)	I2	I4
R1 (brown-black-yellow-gold)	H4	H5
R2 (orange-orange-yellow-gold)	H6	H7
R4 (brown-black-orange-gold)	I5	I11
NXT black-white	X2	H2
Input + –	G11	X11

The voltmeter program converts the Raw sensor value RVal into mV, and displays the result on the NXT display. Because of variations in electrical components, you might need to adjust the exact offset and scale values in Listing 9-4 for your sensor to get the best zero and voltage calibration. Listing 9-5 shows just the main loop of the voltmeter program. To keep precision with the NXT integer math, the scale value is ten times larger than it should be to start with, and the result is divided by ten to make up for it. If you added five before you divided, then it would be the same as rounding the number.

Listing 9-4. *Variable Declarations in Voltmeter Program*

```
RVal sword
Scale sword 16 // approximately 16 but determine experimentally
Offset sword 560 // approximately 560 but determine experimentally
```

Listing 9-5. *Main Loop in Voltmeter Program*

```
Forever:
 getin  RVal, thePort, RawValue  // read in new value
 sub RVal, Offset, RVal //remove offset   RVal = Offset - RVal
 mul RVal, RVal, Scale  //scale to volts  RVal = RVal * Scale
 div RVal, RVal, 10     //adjust to mV    RVal = RVal / 10
 numtostr dtArgs.Text, RVal  // convert number to string
 syscall DrawText, dtArgs    // display number
 gettick nowTick   // what time is it now?
 add    thenTick, nowTick, 100 // wait 100 ms
Waiting:
 gettick nowTick
 brcmp  LT, Waiting, nowTick, thenTick  // time up?
jmp Forever
```

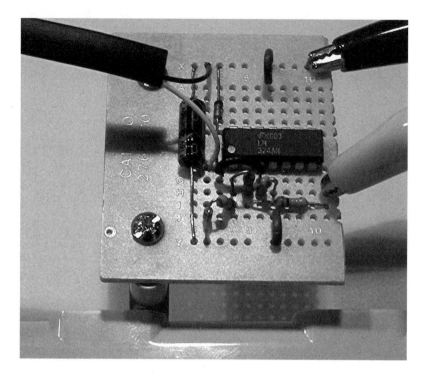

Figure 9-7. *Half-volt sensor on PC board*

Current Sensor

You can use a voltage sensor to measure electrical current by using Ohm's Law. That is V = I × R, where the voltage V equals the current I multiplied by the resistance R. The resistance in this case is of a component known as a shunt resistor. Shunt resistors are connected in series with a circuit, as shown in Figure 9-8, and must have a low resistance so they don't significantly affect the current flowing to the load.

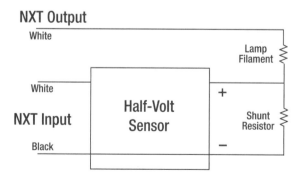

Figure 9-8. *Current sensor circuit*

This shunt resistor is made from four 10Ω resistors in parallel to make a 2.5Ω resistor. You can use a single 2.5Ω resistor, but it's harder to find resistors less than 10Ω. Using Ohm's Law again, you can calculate that 0.2A will be flowing through the 2.5Ω resistor when the voltage is 0.5V. If you want to measure higher currents, you need to use a lower shunt resistor value. For example, with a 1Ω resistor you can measure up to 0.5A.

Electronic Whistler

Back in Chapter 5 you learned that some components, such as thermistors, change resistance value with temperature. An incandescent light bulb filament is another interesting example. When the bulb is cold, the filament resistance is low, but as it heats up to produce light, the resistance increases by more than a factor of ten. It's an interesting example because the heat that's raising the temperature of the filament is coming from the filament itself.

Objects lose heat by convection, conduction, and radiation. Convection is cooling by air moving over an object, and the faster the air moves, the more the cooling. Conduction is loss by touching other objects, and radiation is loss by emitting light or infrared energy. Ordinarily a lamp filament can only radiate energy because it's in a vacuum and it's barely touching anything. You can add convection cooling by removing the glass bulb.

Figure 9-8 shows the half-volt sensor combined with a shunt resistor to measure the current flowing through a lamp filament. If you use a filament from a light bulb intended for household power, it will barely get hot with the paltry 9V the NXT can output. Because the filament isn't very hot, the radiation part of the heat loss is essentially zero. The current will heat the filament to a point where the convection heat loss equals the electrical energy going into it. Because the filament resistance depends on its temperature, a measurement of the current is about like measuring the speed of the wind cooling it. In the scientific world, this instrument is called a hot wire anemometer.

Extracting the Filament

Getting the filament out of a light bulb without destroying it isn't as easy as just breaking the bulb. If you try that, you'll find that the vacuum inside the bulb causes an implosion that sends glass fragments in every direction, tearing the filament to shreds. Instead, you need to let air back into the bulb in a slower, more controlled way.

Caution The following operations are dangerous and require the proper safety measures:

Be careful; wear safety glasses and gloves.

When working with an open flame, make sure there is nothing combustible nearby.

Work where it will be easy to clean up any glass fragments that might fly off.

Make sure you have adult supervision.

The best way to let air gently back into the bulb is to melt a spot on the glass envelope and let the vacuum do the work of sucking a small hole. Figure 9-9 shows a small torch heating the tip of a 40W 120V chandelier bulb. A similar-wattage 240V bulb would probably also work for this. You can use a larger torch intended for soldering plumbing too, but only heat the very tip of the bulb.

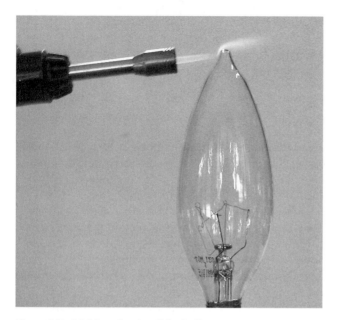

Figure 9-9. *Melting the tip of the bulb*

You can see where the tip of the bulb has turned into a hole in Figure 9-10. It makes a *pop* sound when it does this. The next step is to break the bulb by pinching it in a vise or C-clamp, as shown in Figure 9-11. The bulb has been wrapped in a paper towel to contain the small pieces of glass.

Figure 9-10. *The hole in the glass bulb*

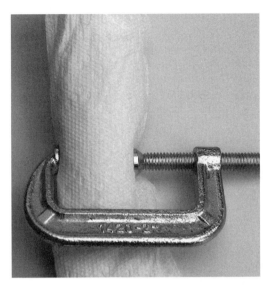

Figure 9-11. *Break the bulb with a C-clamp*

Do not touch the filament or support structure because they're extremely fragile. Remove any remaining pieces of glass with needle-nose pliers (see Figure 9-12), then carefully screw the bulb into its socket.

Figure 9-12. *Remove the remaining glass with needle-nose pliers*

Whistler Construction

The finished electronic whistler is shown in Figure 9-13. Mounted to the side of the NXT, the filament is exposed so you can blow air on it. The whistle NBC program (see Listings 9-6 and 9-7) reads the sensor, displays the value, and produces a whistle tone whose frequency is proportional to the value. As you blow on the filament, the pitch of the tone will increase. Just waving air at the sensor with your hand or moving it around will change the tone.

Figure 9-13. *Finished electronic whistler*

Listing 9-6. *Whistler Declarations*

```
Offset sword 400 // approximately 400 but determine experimentally
```

Listing 9-7. *Central Part of Whistler Program*

```
// turn output port A full power
    setout theOPort, OutputMode, theMode, RunState, rsVal, Power, pwr,
    UpdateFlags, heUF

forever:
 getin  RVal, theIPort, RawValue   // read new value
 sub RVal, Offset, RVal  // RVal = Offset - RVal
```

```
  numtostr dtArgs.Text, RVal  // convert RVal to string
  syscall DrawText, dtArgs    // display on screen
  mul RVal, RVal, 10  // scale up by 10 for wider freq
  mov PT_A.freq, RVal   // set tone freq
  syscall SoundPlayTone, PT_A   // play the tone
jmp forever
```

Pressure Sensor

Back in Chapter 6 you made an elementary pressure sensor using LEGO pneumatics. Now that you can make op-amp circuits, you can make a more accurate sensor using the bridge pressure transducer shown in Figure 9-14. This is a Model 1230-030D-3L PC board mountable pressure transducer from Measurement Specialties (see Table 9-3 for the full bill of materials). It can measure up to 30psi (2,068hPa or 2 Atmospheres), and it reads the difference in pressure between the two ports.

■**Caution** You can only use this sensor to measure the pressure of a gas. Do not try to measure the pressure of liquids or let any moisture get into it.

Figure 9-14. *Bridge pressure transducer*

The pressure transducer is component P1 in the circuit shown in Figure 9-15. Internally it is four resistive elements in an arrangement known as a Wheatstone bridge. With 5V applied to the top of the bridge, the measurement of interest is the difference of the two voltage dividers, and this difference is only 100mV full-scale. Op-amp followers U1B and U1D condition the two voltage-divider values so the differential amplifier made with U1A can subtract and then amplify the difference by ten.

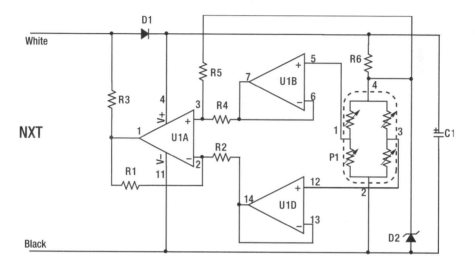

Figure 9-15. *Pressure sensor circuit*

Table 9-3. *Bill of Materials*

Component	Part Number	Description	Radio Shack
U1	LM324	Quad OpAmp	276-1711
D1	1N4148	Small Signal Diode	276-1122
D2	1N4733A	5.1V 1W Zener Diode	276-565
R1	100kΩ	1/4 W 5% Carbon Film Resistor (brown-black-yellow-gold)	271-312 For All Resistors
R2, R4	10kΩ	1/4 W 5% Carbon Film Resistor (brown-black-orange-gold)	See R1
R3	1kΩ	1/4 W 5% Carbon Film Resistor (brown-black-red-gold)	See R1
R5	1megΩ	1/4 W 5% Carbon Film Resistor (brown-black-green-gold)	See R1
R6	470Ω	1/4 W 5% Carbon Film Resistor (yellow-violet-brown-gold)	See R1
P1	1230-030D-3L	Measurement Specialties	Digi-Key MSP6822-ND
C1	22uF	16V or Higher Electrolytic Capacitor	272-1014

Diode D2 is a Zener type diode that creates a constant 5V for the pressure transducer. Resistor R5 offsets the output of U1A so that the sensor can measure negative pressures. Figure 9-16 shows the pressure sensor built on a solderless breadboard, and Table 9-4 has the step-by-step construction of the whole sensor.

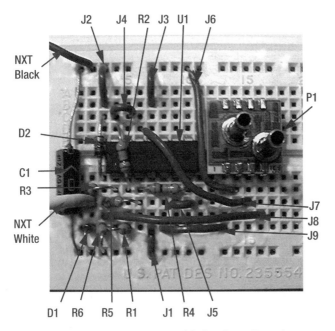

Figure 9-16. *Pressure sensor on solderless breadboard*

Table 9-4. *Component Placement*

Component	Start	End
U1 pin 1	F4	
C1 + −	Y1	X1
J1	Y7	J7
J2	X7	B7
D1 anode cathode	J2	Y2
J3	X3	B3
J4	C4	C5
D2 anode cathode	C3	F3
R2	D4	G5
R3	G2	G4
R4	F10	F6
R1	J5	J4
R6	Y3	J3
R5	H3	H6

continued

Table 9-4. *(continued)*

Component	Start	End
J5	H9	H10
P1 pin 1	F13	
J6	X10	G14
J7	D6	H15
J8	I3	I16
J9	J8	J13
NXT white black	H2	X2

After you've built the pressure sensor, it needs to be calibrated. With nothing connected to the transducer ports, the pressure reading should be zero, because the pressure difference is zero. However, the sensor reading is deliberately offset by a Raw value of approximately 580 so it can measure negative pressures. You can use Boyle's Law to calculate the slope of the relationship between Raw value and pressure. Boyle's Law says that the product of the pressure and volume of a gas is a constant. In other words, if you half the volume of a gas you'll double its pressure.

You can get disposable 10ml oral syringes such as the one shown in Figure 9-17 from pharmacies. Set the syringe for exactly 10ml and connect it to the lower pressure port with a very short piece of LEGO pneumatic or other tubing. There's about 0.5ml of air in the tubing and sensor that is not measured by the syringe, so you need to compress the syringe to 3ml to cut the volume to exactly one-third.

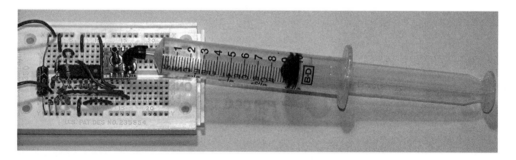

Figure 9-17. *Calibrating the pressure sensor with Boyle's Law*

Boyle's Law says the pressure is now three times as high as it was initially. The initial pressure was atmospheric, which is about 14.7psi (1,014hPa or 1atm), so now it is 44.1psi (3,041hPa or 3atm). The pressure transducer reads the difference between the two ports, and the other port is still seeing atmospheric pressure. So, the pressure sensor should be reading 29.4psi (2,027hPa or 2atm). This should lead to a slope of approximately 6.2 Raw values to 1psi.

When you're done calibrating the sensor, you should be able to generate a plot like the one in Figure 9-18. Listing 9-8 shows the declarations, and Listing 9-9 shows the conversion steps of a pressure sensor NBC program that automatically converts the Raw values to psi and displays the value on the NXT.

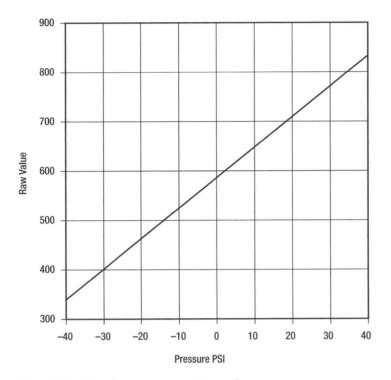

Figure 9-18. *Plot of pressure versus Raw value*

Listing 9-8. *Pressure Program Declarations*

```
Scale sword 6   // approximately 6 but determine experimentally
Offset sword 580 // approximately 580 but determine experimentally
```

Listing 9-9. *Conversion of Raw Value to psi*

```
sub RVal, RVal, Offset //remove offset    RVal = RVal - Offset
div RVal, RVal, Scale  //scale to volts  RVal = RVal / Scale
```

CHAPTER 10

■■■

Aftermarket Vendors

Some sensors are simply too complex to homebrew and others might be too difficult to build because they require electronic components that are too small to handle. Fortunately, several companies have stepped in to provide sophisticated sensors whose market is too small for a big company like LEGO. It isn't our intention to make this chapter look like a product catalog, because over the life of this book many of their offerings will change, but rather to make you aware of other places to look to fill your sensing needs. Links to all the vendors are given in Appendix B.

HiTechnic

At the time of this writing, HiTechnic has a privileged position with LEGO. Due to its third-party licensing agreement, you can purchase its compass sensor (see Figure 10-1) directly from LEGO, and it uses the same plastic enclosure as the genuine NXT sensors. HiTechnic also manufactures a variety of other NXT sensors, such as Color and Acceleration, as well as sensors originally designed for the RCX.

Figure 10-1. *HiTechnic compass sensor mounted on robot*

Mindsensors.com

The products from mindsensors.com look a little like somebody might have homebrewed them. They are printed circuit boards with exposed electronics and mounting holes that have just the right diameter to press-fit blue Technic axle pins into. However, they are professionally designed and manufactured. For example, mindsensors.com's three-axis accelerometer shown in Figure 10-2 can detect the direction of the pull of gravity and could be used to give a walking robot a sense of balance.

Figure 10-2. *Mindsensors.com's three-axis accelerometer*

One particularly notable product mindsensors.com makes isn't a sensor at all. It's a motor output (see Figure 10-3) that provides control for four RCX-style motors complete with pulse width modulation. We wouldn't even dream of homebrewing something this complex. Chapter 12 has amplifier designs that could extend the power capability of an expander such as this to several amps.

Figure 10-3. *Mindsensors.com's four-motor expander*

Techno-Stuff

Techno-stuff is a one-man—Pete Sevcik—operation. He makes RCX-type sensors, but you can use them with the NXT as well. The sensors are painstakingly packaged to look like LEGO bricks. For example, Figure 10-4 is of a unique sensor that reads the pitch or frequency of a tone.

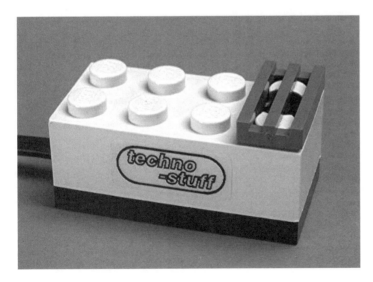

Figure 10-4. *Techno-stuff's pitch sensor*

Vernier and DCP Microdevelopments

Vernier is a scientific devices company that makes a wide variety of instrumentation products for the education market. It sells more than 50 different types of sensors and several data logging products. Because its sensors are designed to have a common interface to go with its data loggers, Vernier can offer an adapter that allows their sensors to be connected to the NXT instead. DCP Microdevelopments also targets the education market. It has a number of sensors and data loggers, although not as extensive a selection as Vernier. Its converter cable was originally designed for the RCX, but the NXT has compatibility with it. So, if you have a special sensing need, it would be worth your while checking with these two companies first to see if they already have the sensor.

LEGO Education

Although not strictly an aftermarket vendor, LEGO Education is an online source for legacy RCX-style sensors and motors as well as the new NXT hardware. It's also a supplier for the DCP sensors and adapter. If you browse in its Parts Product Type, you'll find a large number of LEGO parts you can't get anywhere else, including pneumatic elements.

■■■

CHAPTER 11

NXT Motor Interfaces

The easiest way to extend the reach of your NXT inventions is to use the motors that came with it to operate the electronic controls of appliances and other equipment. The motor simply needs to be mechanically arranged to push the buttons, turn the knobs, or flip the switches on the external device to control it. The NXT motor makes it easy because it has a lot of torque and has built-in position feedback.

The Clapper

Buttons are common controls, and you can arrange the NXT motor to push them instead of you doing it. The exact mechanical design will vary from device to device, but you can operate anything from expensive laboratory equipment to disposable cameras this way. When you push buttons on a remote control, the NXT can practically control the world—at least anything plugged into the wall.

For example, Radio Shack sells a little handheld remote control that transmits to a base station with an electrical outlet in it. All kinds of lights and appliances can be plugged into it. In fact, this is the safest way to control this kind of power, and we highly recommend it. Figure 11-1 shows the handheld remote control and the mechanism used to push the on and off ends of the channel one button. The gears are only being used for their peg holes, not their teeth. The top gear acts as a driver and the lower one as a guide. When the motor turns forward, the linkage pushes the on-end of the button, and when the motor reverses, the off-end.

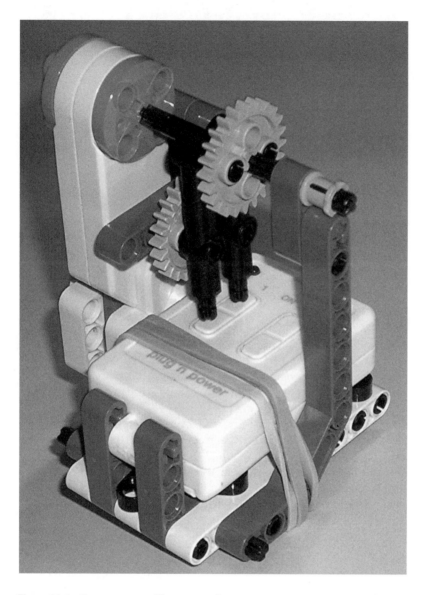

Figure 11-1. *Remote control button pusher*

Figure 11-2 is an NXT-G program to reproduce a simple remote-control product called the Clapper. The Clapper turns something on or off when it hears a loud sound. The program waits till the Sound Sensor picks up a noise louder than 25, then it pulses the motor forward with the Motor block. This pushes the on-end of the remote control button. It then waits for a second loud sound. This time it pulses the motor in reverse, which pushes the off-end of the button. The program loops back and waits for another sound.

Figure 11-2. *The Clapper program*

The buttons don't require a lot of force, so the NXT-G Motor block shown in Figure 11-3 only uses 50% power. A 0.3-second pulse is all that's needed to rotate the mechanism far enough to push the button. Because the Next Action in the Motor block is coast, the motor naturally springs back to a neutral position.

Figure 11-3. *Motor block from button pusher*

The Etch-A-NXT

Volume, tuning, position, brightness, and many other analog controls are rotary types. Designed for human fingertips, they can also be turned with an NXT motor. The built-in position feedback in the NXT motor really comes in handy for this type of control. All you need is a coupler to attach the LEGO axle to the knob of the control you want to turn. The coupler might need to be custom made, but usually gears, pulleys, wheels, or tires can be used to attach the control knob to an axle.

Etch A Sketch is a drawing toy from Ohio Art that uses two knobs to control a cursor that draws a line on a screen. The right knob controls vertical and the left knob controls the horizontal movement of the cursor. Drawing with it is particularly challenging because the cursor always draws a line. You can't just move to a new location and start drawing again. You also need to coordinate the movement of both knobs when you want to draw anything but a straight horizontal or vertical line. You can eliminate this difficulty by driving the knobs with the NXT creating the Etch-A-NXT. Figure 11-4 shows the little assembly that holds the two motors in position. The particular Etch A Sketch in the picture is the pocket version, which is smaller than the original.

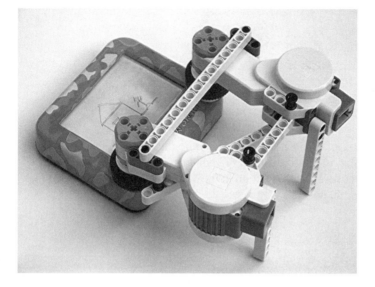

Figure 11-4. *Etch-A-NXT*

Couplers for the knobs are made using the #2994 30.4x14 VR wheels and the #6578 very small balloon tires. These were parts in the original MINDSTORMS Invention Kits, and are found in a variety of LEGO model car kits. One tire rim is on the wheel and the other is on the knob, as shown in Figure 11-5. It grips both well enough to drive the knobs without any slippage. The larger balloon tires that come with the NXT version of the MINDSTORMS kit fit nicely on the knobs on the bigger original Etch A Sketch.

Figure 11-5. *Etch-A-NXT knob coupler*

The NXT-G program shown in Figure 11-6 uses a My Block to take care of reading values from a text file and turning the knobs accordingly. The movements are stored in the text file as relative horizontal and vertical distances. The short wait allows the motors to come to a full stop before continuing on to the next point.

Figure 11-6. *Etch-A-NXT main program loop*

The My Block file_move3 is shown in Figure 11-7. Inside the two File blocks is the name of the text (.txt) file where the distances are stored. You must keep this file name the same in both blocks if you change it. When the last distance has been read, the STOP block is executed, and that ends the program.

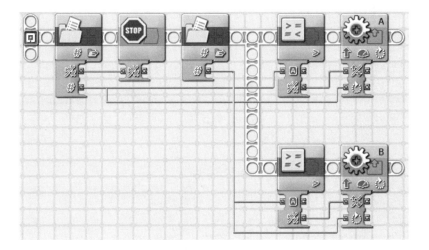

Figure 11-7. *My Block file_move3*

The distances are stored as text, one value per line, with the horizontal distance first, followed by the vertical, as seen in Listing 11-1. You need to use a simple text editor program such as Notepad to generate these files because other word processing programs add unwanted formatting information. Pairs of distances are read and fed in parallel to the Motor blocks. A Motor block ignores the sign or direction of the distance value. The direction of the command is determined by comparing the value to 0 and feeding that logical result to the direction input of the Motor block.

Listing 11-1. *Drawing File Format*

```
Horizontal_1
Vertical_1
Horizontal_2
Vertical_2
Horizontal_3
Vertical_3
...
```

The example drawing file box.txt contains the distance commands to create a simple box that's 200 units on a side (see Listing 11-2). MyFile.txt, available from the book website (go to the Source Code/Download area at http://www.apress.com), is considerably more ambitious. It draws the picture of a house and a waving stickperson next to it shown in Figure 11-8. The text files must be downloaded to the NXT before running the Etch-A-NXT program.

Listing 11-2. *Listing for Drawing File box.txt*

```
200
0
0
200
-200
0
0
-200
```

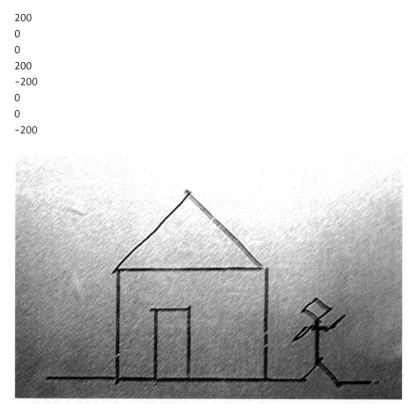

Figure 11-8. *Drawing created from MyFile.txt*

The first step in downloading a drawing text file is to open the NXT window in the NXT-G programming environment. Click on the upper left button in the control cluster shown in Figure 11-9. This brings up the window shown in Figure 11-10 that has two tabs: Communications and Memory. Select the Memory tab, and you'll see the window shown in Figure 11-11 where you need to pick the Other file type under NXT Memory Usage. However, the first time you do this you won't see the Other category. Either way, press the Download button. In the window that opens, you need to change the "Files of type" to include All Files (*.*), or you won't see files with the .txt extension. When you've found the file you want to download to the NXT, just double-click its name.

Figure 11-9. *Button to bring up the NXT window*

Figure 11-10. *NXT Communications and Memory window*

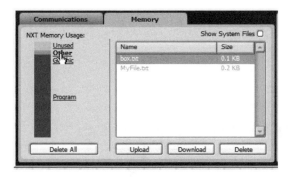

Figure 11-11. *Select the Other file type and download the file to the NXT.*

The Pneumatic Gripper

Toggle switches are another common control device you'll want to operate. LEGO pneumatic cylinders are controlled by toggle-switch–type valves that select one of two tubes that will receive air pressure. Because they're already LEGO components, connecting them to the NXT motor is easy. The switch operator is the same size as a Technic axle, and you can connect a linkage to it, as shown in Figure 11-12, to move it between the two operating points. In the mechanical engineering world, this called a four bar linkage.

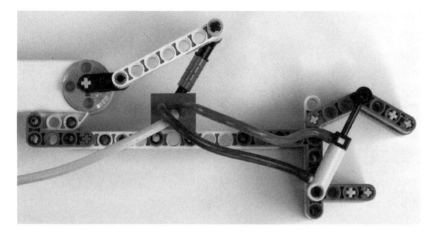

Figure 11-12. *Open pneumatic gripper*

Robotic grippers are a good application for pneumatic control. The force provided by a pneumatic cylinder is gentle, and it's a compact way to deliver the force directly to the jaws. The simple one-sided gripper, shown open in Figure 11-12 and closed in Figure 11-13, is operated by rotating the NXT motor between two positions 180 degrees apart.

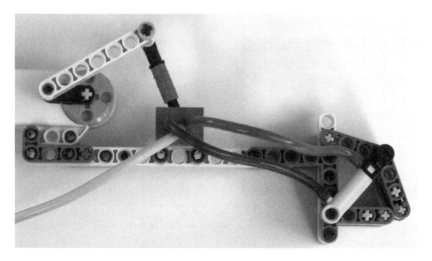

Figure 11-13. *Closed pneumatic gripper*

An NXT-G program to control the gripper is shown in Figure 11-14. Every time you push the left button on the NXT, the motor rotates 180 degrees, and that toggles the gripper open and closed. The details of the Motor block are shown in Figure 11-15, where you can see the 180-degree Duration value. Before running the program, you need to rotate the motor by hand so the valve starts out in one of the two positions.

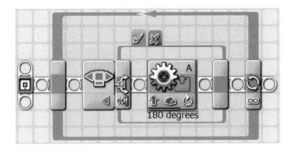

Figure 11-14. *Program to toggle gripper*

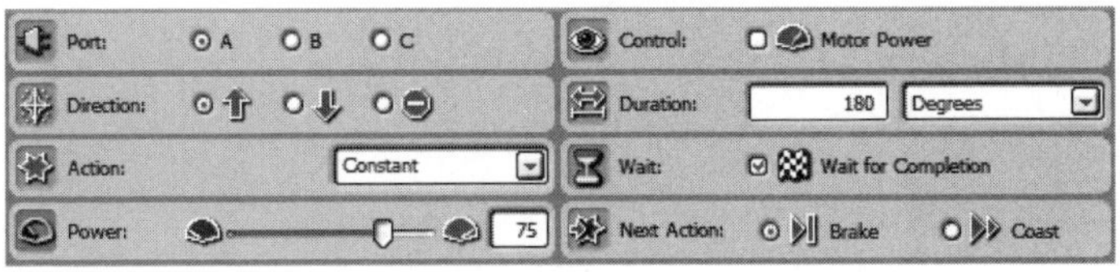

Port:	A	B	C		Control:	Motor Power	
Direction:	↑	↓	⊖		Duration:	180	Degrees
Action:			Constant		Wait:	☑ Wait for Completion	
Power:			75		Next Action:	Brake	Coast

Figure 11-15. *Motor block showing 180-degree movement*

CHAPTER 12

Beyond NXT Motors

The NXT has three output ports with variable power and polarity control that you can use to activate a variety of devices above and beyond the NXT motors. The sophisticated pulse width modulation circuitry behind these ports was already described in Chapter 3. The NXT output power is on the same two wires that we used for passive sensors: the black and the white wires in the NXT cable, or pin 1 and pin 2 on the output port connector. The white wire will be positive and the black negative when the motor output is set to forward. For most of the projects that follow, we'll only show only 18 gauge (0.8mm^2) speaker wires, and you can presume they are attached to these two NXT connections.

The Motor Block

Three NXT-G blocks control the output ports. The Move block is specifically designed for simultaneous control of two outputs for steering vehicles, and is not generally useful for controlling single outputs. The Motor block makes full use of the built-in NXT feedback, while the Motor* block is designed for the older, less-sophisticated LEGO 9V motors. Figure 12-1 shows the Motor block in its expanded form. In this form, a variety of data inputs and outputs are available, but most of these are concerned with the built-in angle feedback. For now, we're only interested in the Power and Direction inputs because they directly control the voltage on the output port.

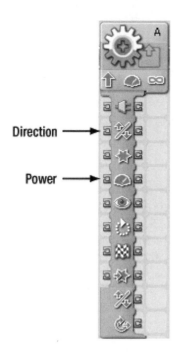

Direction

Power

Figure 12-1. *Expanded Motor block*

Output Control Program

It would be nice if the NXT came with a control panel that allowed you to adjust the output power directly with a "Try Me"–type menu, but it doesn't. The NXT-G program laid out in Figures 12-2, 12-3, and 12-4 is handy for debugging the projects that follow. Pushing the right NXT button increases the motor power up to 100, and pushing the left button decreases the power to –100. A –100 power is actually a power of 100 in reverse.

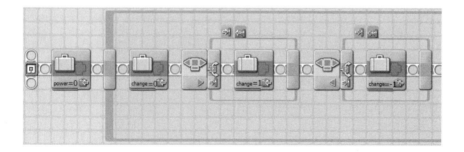

Figure 12-2. *Output control program—initalization and button detection*

The power level is stored in the variable *power*, and the increment amount—+1, 0, or –1—
is stored in the variable *change*. When the value of *power* reaches +101 or –101, you need to set
it back to the limit. The sign of the value of *power* is determined by comparing it to zero. The
result of this comparison becomes the direction input for the Motor block.

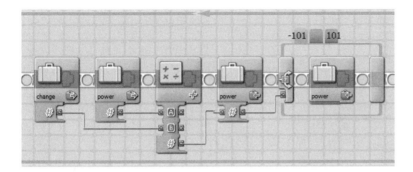

Figure 12-3. *Output control program—change and limit*

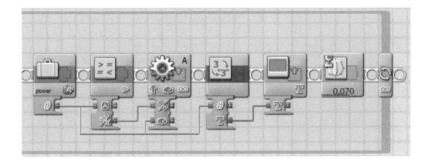

Figure 12-4. *Output control program—output and display*

Lamps

By far, the simplest non-LEGO device you can connect to an NXT output port is an incandescent
lamp. Lamps don't care about polarity, which means you can hook the black and white wires
either way as shown in the circuit diagram in Figure 12-5. About the only problem is that the 9V
output of the NXT is an uncommon voltage for lamps. Higher voltage lamps aren't very bright,
while you can burn out lower voltage lamps by accidentally putting full power to the output.

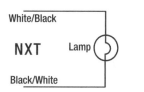

Figure 12-5. *Lamp circuit*

Figure 12-6 shows a small light bulb and plastic socket available at Radio Shack. The lamp is designed to operate from 7.5V, so you shouldn't set Motor block power to more than about 90 to keep from burning it out. Simply screw wires to the two terminals of the socket, and you're ready to create light on command.

Figure 12-6. *7.5V lamp in socket*

Muscle Wires

Muscle Wires are a type of shape memory alloy (SMA) made from an alloy of nickel and titanium called Flexinol. Due to their crystal structure, SMAs change shape at different temperatures. Below a critical transition temperature, Muscle Wires can stretch by as much as eight percent, but they recover their original length when heated. You can use this contraction to create motion without the usual need for motors. You can supply the heat externally or you can generate it internally by passing electrical current through the wire. The time it takes to heat or cool the wire is measured in seconds, and that greatly limits the places where it can be used.

The easiest way to start experimenting with Muscle Wires is to buy the "Muscle Wires Project Book and Sample Kit" from the Jameco Robot Store (Catalog Number: 3-141). Figure 12-7 shows a basic lever demonstration built with one of the Flexinol 150LT wires that comes in the kit. The Muscle Wire runs from the base of the tower to the short side of the lever, and a bag of coins on the long side of the lever provides the force to stretch it. When the NXT output passes current through the Muscle Wire it will be heated, causing it to contract and lift the bag.

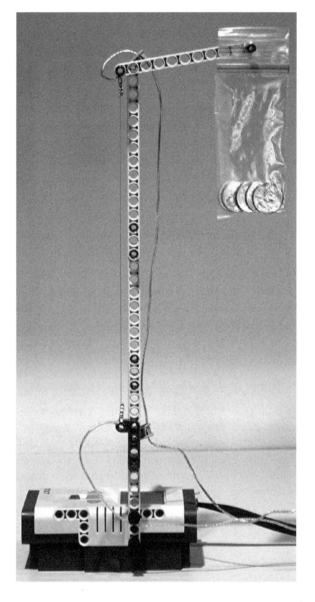

Figure 12-7. *Muscle Wire lever demonstation*

Making good connections to a Muscle Wire is challenging because it's brittle and cannot be soldered. The kit comes with little crimp connectors that are used to fasten the Muscle Wire to an anchor and an electrical wire. Crimp the Muscle Wire to one end of the connector and then crimp a loop of solid hook-up wire the same size as a Technic peg and a length of speaker wire on the other end. While holding the Muscle Wire end of the connector with needle nose pliers to keep it cool, solder the other end with the loop and speaker wire together. When you're done, the connector should look like Figure 12-8. Repeat this for the other end.

Figure 12-8. *Crimp assembly*

You attach the Muscle Wire to the base of the tower and lever using black Technic pegs, as in Figure 12-9. The NXT-G program in Figure 12-10 applies power to the output for five seconds. The power level only needs to be about 25 to get full contraction. The voltage on the wire should be less than 0.3V/cm to prevent it from overheating. Then the program waits five seconds to let the wire cool down and stretch. Audible "Start" and "Stop" sounds are generated with Sound blocks, so you can tell when the NXT is switching the power on and off.

Figure 12-9. *Anchor at base of tower*

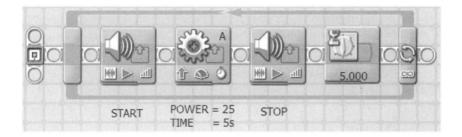

Figure 12-10. *Muscle Wire program*

Electromagnets and Solenoids

A motor is just a fancy kind of electromagnet, and it probably isn't too surprising that you can hook up an electromagnet to an output instead of the NXT motor. A *solenoid* is also an electromagnet that includes a metal rod that moves in and out of the winding, called the *armature*. It's like a motor that goes back and forth rather than around.

Kinetic Sculpture

Normally a swinging pendulum eventually stops due to friction. If a small amount of energy is pumped into the pendulum at the right time, like pushing a child in a swing, it will keep on going. That's the secret behind the kinetic sculpture shown in Figure 12-11. An electromagnet in the base is pulsed on to attract a small metal globe as it swings by. You control the timing by using an NXT Light Sensor to detect when the globe is in the correct position.

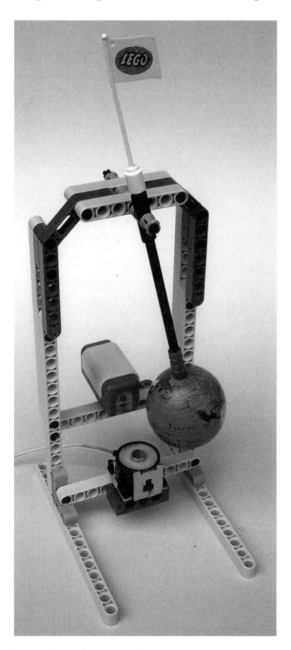

Figure 12-11. *Kinetic sculpture*

The metal globe is from the small toy pencil sharpener shown in Figure 12-12. You can probably find these in the stationery department of a variety store. The mounting hole in the North Pole of the globe is enlarged, and a blue Technic axle peg is pressed into it to allow it to be connected to Technic axle components.

Figure 12-12. *Globe pencil sharpener*

The electromagnet (see Figure 12-13) is a coil removed from a device known as a *relay*. The relay is a Potter and Brumfield KRPA-11DG-6, which has a 6VDC coil (we'll discuss correct use of relays in the following section). It's all right to use a lower-voltage coil because the 9V of the NXT is only briefly applied to the coil, and the voltage is much less than 6V on average. You can attach the coil to the structure with a rubber band or double-face tape.

Figure 12-13. *Electromagnet coil from 6V relay*

The NXT-G program shown in Figure 12-14 loops till the globe casts a shadow on the Light Sensor, making its value less than 50. The program then gives the electromagnet a short pulse on with the Motor block and makes a little click with the Sound block. After that, it waits till the sensor is exposed to the light again as the globe swings past. It keeps looping till the globe swings back from the other direction, which starts the whole process over again.

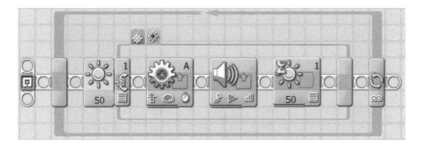

Figure 12-14. *Kinetic sculpture program*

There needs to be enough light in front of the sculpture so that the globe casts a shadow on the Light Sensor. Then you need to start the pendulum swinging by hand. After that, it keeps swinging and making a sound like a metronome. You can use it to provide animation for small objects such as flags or Minifigs.

Relays

Relays are controlled switches that use an electromagnet to move electrical contacts on and off. Usually relays have both normally open (NO) and normally closed (NC) contacts with a shared common connection. The common connection is also known as the *pole*. When the electromagnet is energized, the pole is pulled toward the NO contact to close it, and away from the NC contact to open it. Figure 12-15 shows the basic relay circuit. The load can be a device operating at a different voltage than the NXT, and also something that requires substantially more power than the NXT can deliver.

■**Caution** Although you could use a relay to control household electricity, we strongly advise you to stay away from it. Even the slightest mistake can be lethal. Stay safe by sticking with devices that operate from low voltages, and preferably from batteries.

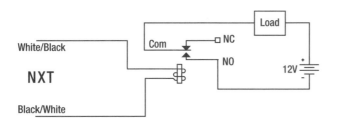

Figure 12-15. *Basic relay circuit*

One of the most important characteristics of a relay is its coil voltage. Just like with light bulbs, 9V is a fairly uncommon voltage for relay coils. Even if you could find a 9V relay, the output voltage of an NXT with weak batteries would be too low to operate it. Your best bet is to buy a 6V relay and operate the NXT output with less than full power. Limit the power value in the Motor block to 80 to keep the voltage on the relay coil around 6V.

The Potter and Brumfield KRPA-11DG-6 is an excellent choice for a relay, but it's expensive and requires an additional octal socket that will add a lot of cost to your project. A good alternative is the Potter and Brumfield PE014006, which is substantially smaller and cheaper. It's designed for mounting on a printed circuit board, but you can solder wires directly to the pins, as shown in Figure 12-16.

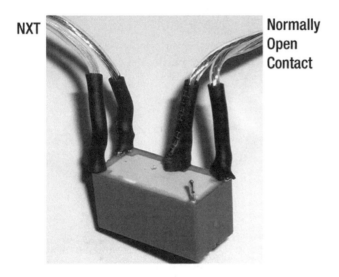

Figure 12-16. *Relay*

Relays are good for operating devices that were originally designed for automotive or marine applications. The NXT is a real weakling compared to equipment that operates at up to 13.8VDC with several amps of current. An automobile vacuum cleaner could be the basis of your own robotic vacuum cleaner. Portable air compressors can supply a constant source of pressure for pneumatics. Boat bilge pumps, as in Figure 12-17, can move liquids in hydroponic gardens or water fountains. It's more economical to run these devices with power supplies that deliver 12V from household electricity, but it's much safer to use batteries.

Figure 12-17. *Relay control of a 12V bilge pump*

Doubling Outputs

Diodes are the one-way valves of the electrical world. The physical package and circuit symbol are shown in Figure 12-18. They have two leads like a resistor, but unlike the resistor the leads are not interchangeable. A diode has an anode and a cathode lead, and a line is painted on the cathode end of the part. Electrical current can only flow from the anode to the cathode. In that direction, the diode looks about like a solid piece of wire. However, in the reverse direction, the diode looks like an open circuit.

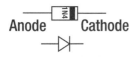

Figure 12-18. *Diode and circuit symbol*

If you connect a diode in series with a light bulb, as in Figure 12-19, then it will only light when the current flow is in one direction and not the other. Because you can control the polarity of the NXT output using the direction input on the Motor block, the bulb will light only in forward or reverse, but not both.

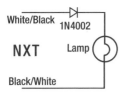

Figure 12-19. *Diode and lamp circuit diagram*

An inexpensive way to get small lights is to cut apart long strings of tiny Christmas tree lights. Up to 50 of these lights are connected in series, which means each light only operates on a few volts. You should only set the power in the Motor block to a low value such as 20, or you'll burn out the light.

Figure 12-20 shows how to connect the diode in series with the light. It's a good idea to solder the connections to make them more permanent. Figure 12-21 shows how you can cover the entire diode and the connections with heat shrink tubing to insulate and protect them.

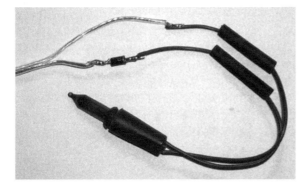

Figure 12-20. *Christmas tree light with diode*

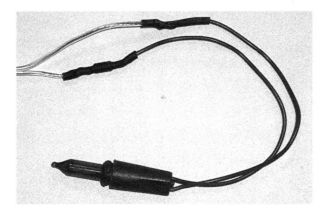

Figure 12-21. *Heat shrink tubing covers the diode and connections*

The whole idea of connecting a diode in series might sound pretty useless, but there is a method to our madness. If you connect two lights to the same output with diodes facing in opposite directions, like the schematic in Figure 12-22, one lamp will light in forward and the other in reverse. In a way, you've doubled the number of NXT outputs because you can control six different lights. The only drawback is that you can only light one light per output at a time.

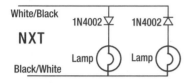

Figure 12-22. *Two lights connected to one output*

Many different types of diodes are available. The best ones to use for NXT outputs are the 1N400X rectifier diodes. The X in the model number has to do with the voltage capability of the part, and the higher the number, the higher the voltage. All of them can handle the current and voltages present on an NXT output. In this book we show the 1N4002, which is good to 100V.

When controlling anything but a resistive load such as a lamp or Muscle Wire, the circuit gets a little more complicated. Figure 12-23 shows how you should add an additional diode to the circuit when operating motors or relays. It's beyond the scope of this book to explain exactly why this diode is necessary, but it has to do with diverting energy that's stored in motors and electromagnets when they get turned off. Not using it will probably damage the other diode. Just like with the lights earlier, now you can control six different motors or relays.

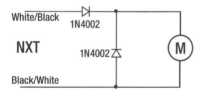

Figure 12-23. *Motor or relay circuit diagram*

You can combine the contacts from two relays controlled by the same output to get voltage polarity control on an output. Figure 12-24 has two of the circuits in Figure 12-23 and an arrangement of relay contacts that switch 12V on the motor to make it go forward with Relay 1 energized, or reverse with Relay 2.

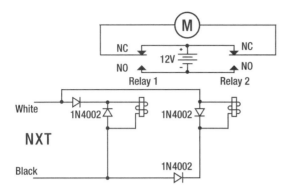

Figure 12-24. *Directional voltage control using two relays*

Although you could use the point-to-point wiring schemes shown so far, it's better to build the circuit shown in Figure 12-24 on a printed circuit board (PCB). Figure 12-25 shows how you can connect the relays and diodes in a sturdy and compact way on a prototype PCB. Speaker wires are used to input the 12V and NXT signals and output the load voltage.

Figure 12-25. *Directional voltage control assembly*

Light Emitting Diodes

Figure 12-26 shows the typical package of a Light Emitting Diode (LED) and its electrical circuit symbol. The symbol is the same as the diode we've already discussed, except for two little arrows that symbolize the light being emitted. Instead of a painted line to signify the cathode end of the LED, like a conventional diode, the LED has a flat space in the flange directly next to that lead. The anode lead is also a little longer than the cathode lead.

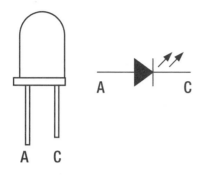

Figure 12-26. *LED outline and circuit symbol*

An LED needs a resistor connected in series with it to limit the amount of current flowing through it. Unlike an incandescent lamp, the voltage across the LED is fixed and only about two volts. If you connect an LED to a voltage greater than that, it won't just shine brightly, it will be permanently damaged.

The calculation of the resistor value is a little mathematical. The first thing you need to know is the power supply voltage from which you intend to run the LED. In the case of the NXT, the output voltage is 9V. The second thing you need to know is the LED voltage drop, and that depends on the particular LED you have. Table 12-1 shows typical values, but it's better to check the datasheet for your particular device. Finally, you need the amount of current that should flow through the LED. That should also come from the datasheet, but Table 12-1 also has typical values.

Subtract the LED voltage from the power supply voltage and then divide the result by the LED current. For example, suppose you have a 9V power supply, a 2V LED voltage drop, and you want 20mA (0.020A) of current. The calculated resistor value is 350Ω, but you would need to use a 330Ω resistor because that's the closest standard resistor value.

$$R = \frac{V - VDrop}{I} \ [\Omega]$$

$$R = \frac{9 - 2}{0.02} = 350 \ [\Omega]$$

Table 12-1. *Typical LED Data*

Color	V Drop	Current	R
Red	1.7 V	20mA	330Ω
High-efficiency red	1.9	20	330
Orange and yellow	2	20	330
Green	2.1	20	330
White, blue, and pure green	3.4	25	220

LEDs only produce light when they are *forward biased*. That means the current needs to flow in the same direction as the arrow of the diode in the LED symbol. This also means the anode voltage must be positive with respect to the cathode. LEDs don't produce light when they are connected backwards or reverse biased. In fact, they can be damaged if the reverse voltage is greater than about 5V. Because the NXT output voltage polarity can be positive or negative, you must protect the LED with another diode to prevent it from being damaged this way.

Figure 12-27 shows the circuit diagram of an LED output, and Figure 12-28 shows the assembly. The value of resistor R is computed using the equation, and the 1N4148 is a small diode used to protect the LED from reverse voltage. You could use a 1N4002, but the 1N4148 is smaller and more appropriate for the current in the LED. Hooking the white NXT cable wire to the resistor and the black to the LED cathode will make an LED that lights when the Motor block output is set to forward. Reversing the white and black connections will make an LED that lights when the Motor block is in reverse.

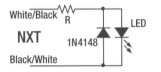

Figure 12-27. *Basic LED circuit*

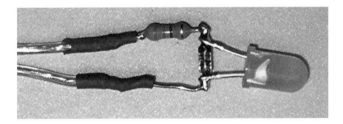

Figure 12-28. *LED assembly*

You can also use another LED in place of the 1N4148, as shown in the circuit in Figure 12-29. They can share the same series resistor if the LEDs are similar enough. Only one LED will light at a time: LED1 when the Motor block output is in forward and LED2 when it is in reverse. Use LEDs in the T13/4 package, which is about 5mm in diameter, because they can be pushed part way into Technic holes for mounting, as in Figure 12-30.

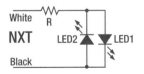

Figure 12-29. *Two-LED circuit*

Figure 12-30. *T13/4 LEDs in Technic beam*

It's easier to create the parallel connection between the LEDs by bending one lead of each LED over to the other LED. Make sure the LEDs are mounted with the cathode flat spot on opposite sides. This gives you two leads to connect to that are separated by enough distance that they won't easily touch and short. Figure 12-31 shows the parallel connection, while Figure 12-32 shows the addition of the series resistor. Finally, Figure 12-33 shows heat shrink covering the connections.

Figure 12-31. *LEDs connected in parallel*

Figure 12-32. *Add common series resistor*

Figure 12-33. *Heat shrink to insulate connections*

Assuming executives make important decisions that are about as good as flipping a coin, you can make a contraption that makes yes/no decisions at the push of a button (see Figure 12-34). You make the yes/no indicator using the circuit shown in Figure 12-28, with one red and one green LED.

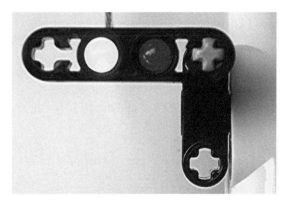

Figure 12-34. *A favorable decision*

The NXT-G program is shown in Figure 12-35. Pushing the center button on the NXT turns the output off, clearing the previous decision. When the button is released, the Random block picks a number 0 or 1, with equal probability. Depending on the number, the output is either turned on in forward or reverse, making either the green/yes or the red/no light up. If you reduce the power level in the Motor block, you could also use two Christmas tree lights connected as in Figure 12-22.

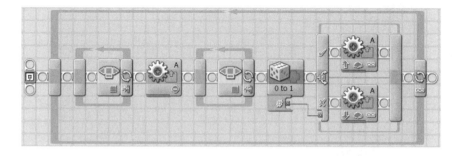

Figure 12-35. *Decision maker program*

More Power

Relays are great for turning on and off equipment that requires power beyond the capability of the NXT. The NXT creates variable power by turning on and off the output thousands of times a second, but relays are way too slow to be operated this way. You can use a solid-state device known as a metal oxide semiconductor field effect transistor (MOSFET) like a relay, but it can switch as fast as the NXT. Unlike relay contacts, the MOSFET only conducts in one direction, so it's only useful for DC applications.

One MOSFET Amplifier

Figure 12-36 shows the basic N-channel MOSFET amplifier using the IRF510. The MOSFET is the complicated symbol in the center of the drawing. It has three leads: the gate, source, and drain. The diode in the symbol is usually not drawn for simplicity, but it's always a part of the device. When the voltage between the gate and source is greater than about 4V, the MOSFET will switch the connection between the drain and the source on. The 10k resistor prevents the gate voltage from floating around when it isn't connected to anything, and the 1N4002 is there to divert the power stored in the motor when it is turned off.

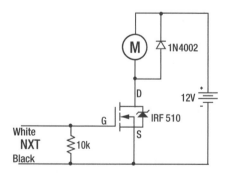

Figure 12-36. *MOSFET unipolar amplifier circuit*

The IRF510 comes in the TO-220AB package shown in Figure 12-37. The drain is connected to both the center lead and the large flange. You can use a small screw and nut to turn the flange into a handy terminal for connecting the load. However, if you need for the IRF510 to carry more than about 2A, you'll need to attach a heat sink to the flange.

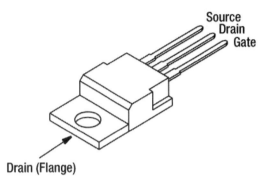

Figure 12-37. *MOSFET package*

A terminal strip version of the MOSFET amplifier is shown in Figure 12-38. The drain lead is bent up and out of the way because the flange is used to make the connection. The wires to the load are soldered to the leads of the 1N4002 to make connecting easier. Make sure you have the cathode (end with the band) of the diode toward the positive power terminal.

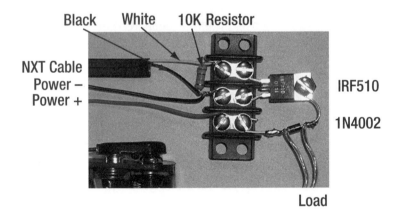

Figure 12-38. *MOSFET amplifier assembly built on a terminal strip*

Because you often need variable speed, motors are the natural application for the MOSFET amplifier. Figure 12-39 shows an automobile electric window motor connected to the amplifier. A variety of motors such as this are used in automobiles for power equipment and windshield wipers. They are geared down much like the NXT motor, but they often use a worm gear that locks the shaft when the motor isn't turning.

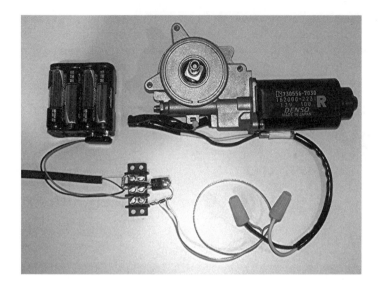

Figure 12-39. *MOSFET amplifier controlling an automotive electric window motor*

Bipolar MOSFET Amplifier

You can vary motor speed with the one MOSFET amplifier, but not the direction. This can be a serious shortcoming for vehicle designs where you need to go both forward and reverse. Extending the design to control both speed and direction requires the more complicated bipolar amplifier shown in Figure 12-40. See Table 12-2 for the bill of materials.

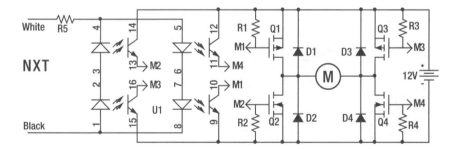

Figure 12-40. *Bipolar amplifier*

Table 12-2. *Bill of Materials*

Component	Part Number	Description	Digi-Key
Q1, Q3	IRF9530PBF	P Chan MOSFET	IRF9530PBF-ND
Q2, Q4	IRF520NPBF	N Chan MOSFET	IRF520NPBF-ND
R1–R4	330 Ohm	1/2 W Resistor	PPC330BCT-ND
R5	100 Ohm	1/4 W Resistor	P100CACT-ND
U1	PS2501-4	NEC Quad Optoisolator	PS2501-4A-ND
D1–D4	STTH2R06RL	Fast Recovery Rectifier Diode	497-4409-1-ND

The heart of the design is the H-bridge made from four MOSFETs. You can see the H pattern where the motor symbol M is in the middle of the horizontal line of the letter H. The upper MOSFETs—Q1 and Q3—are P-channel, while the lowers—Q2 and Q4—are N-channel like the IRF510. P-channel MOSFETs work like their N-channel brothers, but have a negative gate voltage. The arrow in the gate part of the symbol is reversed to differentiate it from the N-channel.

You use the MOSFETs in pairs to connect either the positive voltage or ground to either end of the motor. The forward pair is Q1 and Q4, and the reverse is Q3 and Q2. U1 is an optoisolator that contains four LEDs and four phototransistors. When the light from an LED shines on a corresponding phototransistor, it turns on. The LEDs are cleverly arranged to turn on the right pairs of MOSFETS to preserve the polarity of the NXT output voltage.

You should first build the bipolar amplifier on a solderless prototype board, and then transfer the working design over to a matching prototype PCB. Figure 12-41 shows the first step in populating the prototype board. Follow Table 12-3 for step-by-step construction, making sure every part is in the correct hole. The MOSFET legs fit tightly in the prototype board and require gentle rocking to minimize the insertion force. Pay special attention to the direction of the diodes—it's easy to connect them backwards accidentally.

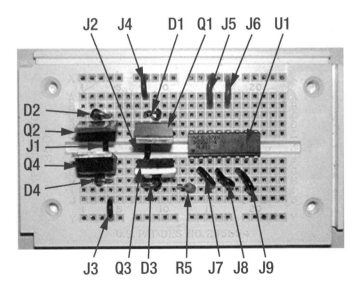

Figure 12-41. *Step one*

Table 12-3. *Component Placement Step One*

Component	Start	End
Q2 Gate Drain Source	D2	D4
J1	E4	F4
Q4 Gate Drain Source	G2	G4
D2 Anode Cathode	C4	C3
D4 Anode Cathode	H4	H3
Q1 Gate Drain Source	D10	D8
J2	E8	F8
Q3 Gate Drain Source	G10	G8
D1 Anode Cathode	C9	C8
D3 Anode Cathode	H9	H8
J3	X8	A8
U1 Pin 1	F13	
J4	J4	Y4
R5	I12	I13
J5	X15	B15
J6	X17	B17
J7	G14	H15
J8	G16	H17
J9	G18	H19

Figure 12-42 shows additional parts, with Table 12-4 giving the step-by-step construction that goes with it. Notice that resistors R1–R4 need to be the larger 1/2 W type because of the power they dissipate. Finally, Figure 12-43 shows the complete circuit with connections to 12V, the NXT, and the load. Again, step-by-step instructions are in Table 12-5.

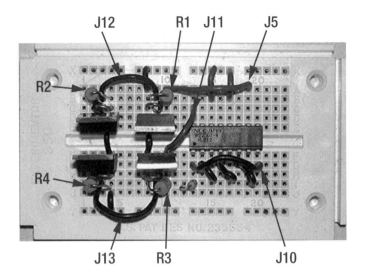

Figure 12-42. *Step two*

Table 12-4. *Component Placement Step Two*

Component	Start	End
R2	B2	B4
J12	B3	B9
R1	B8	B10
R4	I2	I4
J13	I3	I9
R3	I8	I10
J11	A10	A19
J10	G13	G20
J14	C13	F10

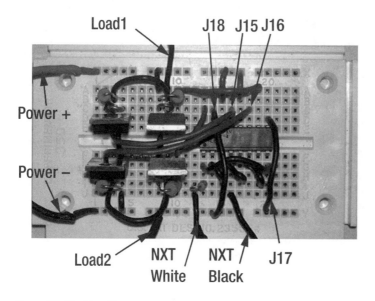

Figure 12-43. *Step three*

Table 12-5. *Component Placement Step Three*

Component	Start	End
Power +12V GND	X1	Y1
Load 1 Load 2	A9	J9
J18	C14	Y14
J17	D20	Y20
J15	C16	E2
J16	C18	F2
NXT White Black	J12	J16

Double-check your connections before connecting the 12V to the circuit. Connect the motor and then the 12V, but not the NXT. The motor should not run and the circuitry should remain cool. When the circuit passes that test, connect the NXT and run the power control program discussed earlier. With a power level of about 10, you should hear the high-pitched noise of the PWM coming from the motor. By the time you advance the power to 50, the motor should be turning. The circuit should operate the same way for negative power, except that the motor will turn in the opposite direction.

You could use the amplifier built on the prototype board, but moving it to a PCB will make it much more reliable. Figure 12-44 shows the final assembly, where components were moved one at a time from the prototype board. The amplifier is capable of controlling up to 15V at 2A without additional heat sinks.

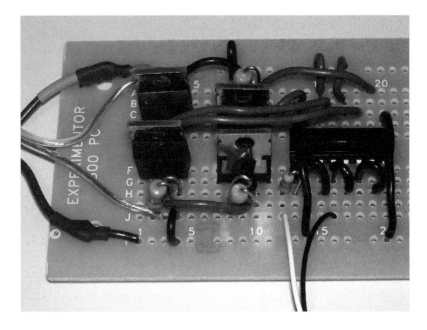

Figure 12-44. *Step four*

The bipolar amplifier is well suited for controlling motors for vehicle propulsion. Figure 12-45 shows a good-sized 24VDC motor that runs nicely on 13.8V from a lead acid battery–based power supply. Generally you don't need the high speed of a DC motor, so it's better to buy motors with built-in gear reduction, called *gear head motors*, because they already have lower speed and higher torque. However, you can lower the ratio externally with drive belts where the smaller pulley, like the one in Figure 12-45, is on the motor and the larger one is on the axle connected to the wheel.

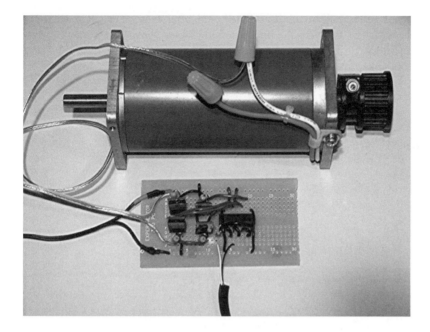

Figure 12-45. *Bipolar amplifier connected to DC motor*

CHAPTER 13

■■■

I²C Bus Communication

The I²C bus is a powerful feature of the NXT because it provides the NXT with practically unlimited expansion capability. Although it's located on the input port connector, it's actually used for expanding both inputs and outputs. Only two wires are necessary because the data is transmitted serially, or one bit at a time. One wire is sending and receiving data (SDA), and the other is providing a clock (SCL). On the input port connector, SDA is pin 6 and SCL is pin 5, or blue and yellow in the NXT cable. You need a third wire for ground, which is either pin 2 or 3, black or red in the NXT cable.

Note The original NXT firmware had some problems with I²C communications, so make sure you're running at least version 1.04 firmware before trying any of these projects. Should your I²C programs appear to hang or crash, cycle the power to the I²C hardware by unplugging and then plugging the sensor port connector back in.

I²C Communications

Fortunately, the NXT takes care of the low-level details of using I²C, but you still need to understand a few things. An I²C bus has one master—the NXT—and up to 127 slave devices. However, there is a practical hardware limit of about eight slaves for the NXT. Each slave has a unique seven-bit address. When the NXT wants to communicate with a device, it sends the address and a single bit to tell whether it wants to read or write. Then the device replies with a single-bit acknowledgement. If the master is writing the device, the data follows right after the acknowledgement. If the NXT is reading the device, it expects the slave to start sending the data immediately. You can also combine the functions to have a write followed immediately by a read. Figure 13-1 shows the transfers graphically.

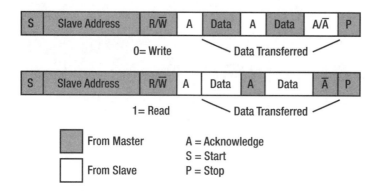

Figure 13-1. *I²C protocol*

PCF8574

One of the most useful I²C devices is the PCF8574 remote I/O expander. It's a single integrated circuit that includes eight pins that can be either inputs or outputs. Figure 13-2 shows the basic block diagram of the part, where the eight I/O pins are labeled P0 to P7. The figure doesn't show the part's interrupt pin because you won't be using it.

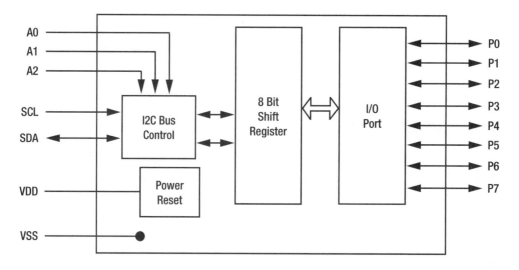

Figure 13-2. *PCF8574*

You use address lines A0, A1, and A2 to generate one of eight possible addresses for the expander. That means you can have eight PCF8574s on the same I²C bus by connecting the address pins either high to VDD, or low to VSS. A PCF8574 with all address lines tied to VSS will have the address 40 hexadecimal (0x40). There's an alternate version of the part with an "A" suffix that has a base address of 70 hexadecimal (0x70). Figure 13-3 illustrates how to compute the address for the two devices.

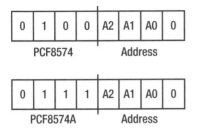

Figure 13-3. *PCF8574 and PCF8574A address*

When used as outputs, the pins can only sink current. That means they can only be expected to pull a load to ground. This can be confusing, because turning a load on means you must write a zero to the pin, not a one. For example, writing a zero will light an LED whose anode is tied to the positive power supply through a resistor. Each output can sink 25mA, and is latched. If your program crashes, they'll remain in whatever state they were in. Fortunately, when first powered up, the default condition of the pins is high, and the loads will be off.

Eight Outs

Figure 13-4 shows a PCF8574 driving eight LEDs. The LEGO hardware documentation specifies that resistors R1 and R2 must be 82kΩ to terminate the I²C bus properly. Rather than using eight discrete LEDs, you can use a single bar graph display that has multiple LEDs in the same package. This particular display has the anodes of ten LEDs along the side with the little notch cut in the corner.

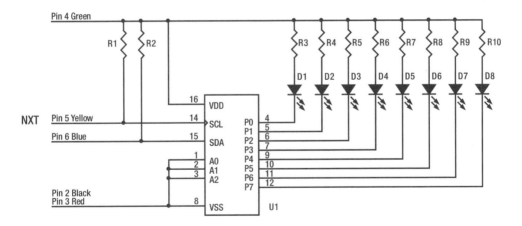

Figure 13-4. *Eight Outs circuit*

Table 13-1 has the complete list of parts you'll need, and Table 13-2 takes you through the placement on the solderless breadboard step by step. Figure 13-5 shows the completed construction. To simplify the wiring, resistors R3 to R10 have insulation stripped from hook-up wire slid over their leads to prevent them from shorting to each other. The solderless breadboard lacks a hole at column 18 where one of the display pins needs to go. Bend the appropriate pin of the display over to an adjacent pin and wrap it around to make its connection.

Table 13-1. *Eight Outs Bill of Materials*

Component	Part Number	Description	Digi-Key
U1	PCF8574	I²C Digital Port	296-13109-5-ND
D1–8	LED	LED Bar Graph Display	160-1068-ND
R1 and R2	82kΩ	1/4 W 1% Film Resistor	P82.0KCACT-ND
R3–R10	150Ω for Eight Outs or 100Ω for Wand	1/4 W 1% Film Resistor	P150CACT-ND or P100CACT-ND

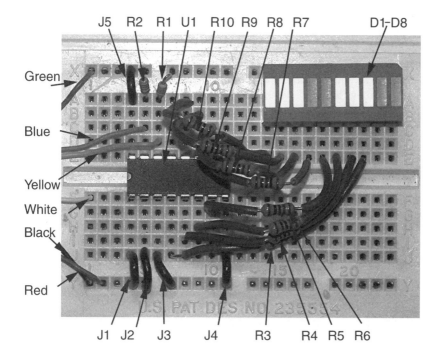

Figure 13-5. *Eight Outs circuit on solderless breadboard*

Table 13-2. *Eight Outs Component Placement*

Component	Start	End
U1 pin 1	F4	
R1	A6	X7
R2	A5	X5
J1	Y4	J4
J2	Y5	J5
J3	Y7	J6
J4	Y11	J11
J5	X4	A4
NXT Green White	X1	H1
NXT Red Black	Y2	Y1

Component	Start	End
NXT Blue Yellow	C5	C6
R3	J7	E21
R4	I8	E20
R5	H9	E19
R6	G10	E18
R7	D11	E17
R8	C10	E16
R9	B9	E15
R10	A8	E14
D1–D8 Anodes on X	X23	

Most likely, if you're using I²C communications, you've outgrown NXT-G. Listing 13-1 is for an NBC program that simply counts and outputs an eight-bit binary number to the display. The system call to CommLSWrite only starts the transmission of data. You need to wait in a loop till the status shows that all the data has been sent to continue. The least significant bit on P0 blinks so fast it only looks dim. The most significant bit on pin P7 takes nearly two seconds to turn on and back off again.

Listing 13-1. *Blinkall.nbc Program*

```
#include "NXTDefs.h"
#define I2CPort IN_1
#define I2CAddress 0x40
// 0x40 for PCF8574 or 0x70 for PCF8574A
dseg    segment
  lswArgs TCommLSWrite        // Write structure
  lscsArgs TCommLSCheckStatus // Status structure
  Value byte
dseg ends
thread main
// Initialize variables
   mov lswArgs.Port, I2CPort
   mov lscsArgs.Port, I2CPort
// Initialize input port to I2C
   SetSensorType(I2CPort,IN_TYPE_LOWSPEED)
   SetSensorMode(I2CPort,IN_MODE_RAW)
   ResetSensor(I2CPort)
Loop:  // Top of loop
// Build buffer and write port
   arrbuild lswArgs.Buffer, I2CAddress, Value
   set lswArgs.ReturnLen, 0 // Read back 0 bytes
   syscall CommLSWrite, lswArgs
Wait: // Wait till done
   syscall CommLSCheckStatus, lscsArgs
```

```
    brtst GT, Wait, lscsArgs.Result
// Increment
    add Value, Value, 1
// Start over
    jmp Loop
endt
```

Magic Wand

If you move the bar graph display back and forth fast enough while changing the pattern, then it will give the appearance of a multicolumn display. That's the magic behind the next project. You've probably seen digital clocks and message displays that work on the same principle.

All you need is the Eight Outs circuit with the display mounted on a separate little integrated-circuit breadboard such as the Radio Shack #27-159 shown in Figure 13-6. We've broken with tradition a little here and mounted the PCF8574 on one of the little boards as well. Allow enough connection wire between the boards so the display will be able to move freely. The 100Ω LED resistors are soldered in series with the connection wire and covered with heat shrink tubing. The lower resistance value makes the display a little brighter and easier to see. However, there's a 180mA limit to current you can draw from the 4.3V power supply.

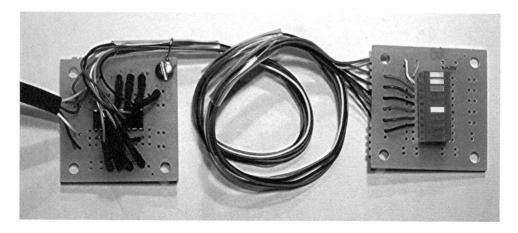

Figure 13-6. *Magic wand on printed circuit*

The spacing of the mounting holes in the PCB allows you to connect it directly to a LEGO beam with small screws and nuts. The simple contraption shown in Figure 13-7 just waves the beam back and forth as fast as it can. You use the touch switch to tell the program when the beam has advanced to the far left end of its travel and is ready to start spelling out the message.

Figure 13-7. *The magic wand*

If you want a large display, use discrete LEDs and mount them to a beam, as shown in Figure 13-8. The display can be much brighter because more efficient LEDs are available in discrete packages than the bar graph displays. Figure 13-9 shows the longer wand in action. The program is exactly the same.

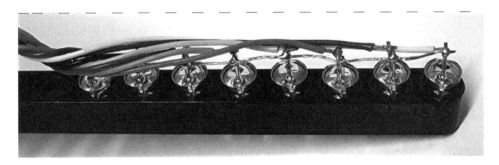

Figure 13-8. *Close-up of wand construction*

Figure 13-9. *Longer magic wand with discrete LEDs*

The complete NBC program listing for the Magic Wand is in Appendix C. Listing 13-2 shows just the part that has to do with generating the data patterns for the letters. Only L, E, G, and O are already in the program, but you can generate any pattern you want that's eight segments high and up to 15 segments long. It's easy to lay out the pattern on graph paper and then convert the pattern to hexadecimal numbers where ones are the lit LEDs. For example, 0x80 would only be the lowest segment lit and 0xFF would be all segments.

Listing 13-2. *Magic Wand Pattern Declarations*

```
// Display patterns
// Each byte represents a column of dots with last byte = 0
// Bit set to 1 means lit LED.
// Least significant bit is at top of column.
// Maximum number of bytes per pattern: 15
   L_ byte[] 0xff, 0x80, 0x80, 0x80, 0x80, 0x80, 0x80, 0x80, 0
   E_ byte[] 0xff, 0x89, 0x89, 0x89, 0x89, 0x81, 0x81, 0x81, 0
   O_ byte[] 0x7e, 0x81, 0x81, 0x81, 0x81, 0x81, 0x81, 0x7e, 0
   G_ byte[] 0x7e, 0x81, 0x81, 0x81, 0x81, 0x91, 0x90, 0x72, 0
```

Four Ins and Outs

It might be exaggerating a little, but the circuit in Figure 13-10 more than doubles the number of inputs and outputs on the NXT—that is, if you only wanted to have switch-type inputs and LED-type outputs—but it is the basic circuit you can use to expand the NXT for other things.

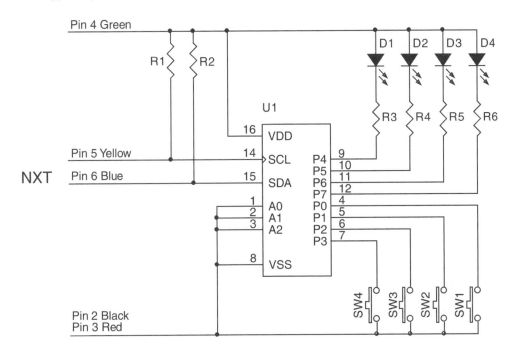

Figure 13-10. *Four Ins and Outs schematic*

The most important thing to see in Figure 13-10 is how the inputs work. Although the PCF8574 can't source current, it does have some weak pull-up resistors built in. If you want to use a pin for input, you must make sure you have written a one to it first. Then all an input device needs to do is pull the pin down to VSS. Much like the outputs, this might be confusing because an input that is on is actually read as a zero.

Table 13-3 is the complete bill of materials, and the step-by-step construction instructions are in Table 13-4. The circuit built on a solderless breadboard is shown in Figure 13-11. The little circuit-board mount buttons are called "tact" switches and are really handy for building projects like this.

Table 13-3. *Four Ins and Outs Bill of Materials*

Component	Part Number	Description	Digi-Key
U1	PCF8574	I²C Digital Port	296-13109-5-ND
D1–D4	LED	4 Different Color LEDs	
R1 and R2	82kΩ	1/4 W 1% Film Resistor	P82.0KCACT-ND
R3–R6	150Ω	1/4 W 1% Film Resistor	P150CACT-ND
SW1–SW4	Tact Switches	PCB NO Switches	EG2495-ND

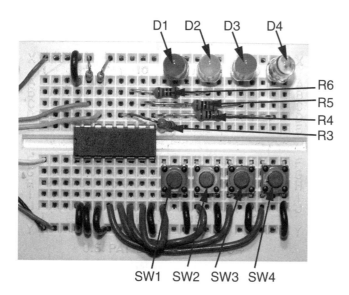

Figure 13-11. *Four Ins and Outs on solderless breadboard*

Table 13-4. *Four Ins and Outs Component Placement*

Component	Start	End
U1 pin 1	F4	
R1	A6	X7
R2	A5	X5
R6	D11	D22
R5	C10	C19
R4	B9	B16
R3	D8	E13
J1	Y4	J4
J2	Y5	J5
J3	Y7	J6
J4	Y11	J11
J5	X4	A4
J6	Y14	J14

Component	Start	End
J7	Y17	J17
J8	Y20	J20
J9	Y23	J23
D1 Anode Cathode	X13	A13
D2 Anode Cathode	X16	A16
D3 Anode Cathode	X19	A19
D4 Anode Cathode	X22	A22
J10	J7	J21
J11	J8	J18
J12	J9	J15
J13	J10	J12
SW1	I21	I23
SW2	I18	I20
SW3	I15	I17
SW4	I12	I14
NXT Green White	X1	H1
NXT Red Black	Y2	Y1
NXT Blue Yellow	C5	C6

The Low2High NBC program just maps whatever is input on the lower four bits to the upper four bits of the PCF8574. It's useful for testing the Four Ins and Outs circuit. Listing 13-3 shows the code for the program. Just after the label called Loop is where the important work gets done. When you set the variable lswArgs.ReturnLen to one, the I²C hardware knows both to write the buffer and to read back one byte. The lower nibble of that byte contains the state of the four switches.

Listing 13-3. *Low2High.nbc Program*

```
#include "NXTDefs.h"
#define I2CPort IN_1
#define I2CAddress 0x40
// 0x40 for PCF8574 or 0x70 for PCF8574A
dseg    segment
  lswArgs TCommLSWrite        // Write structure
  lscsArgs TCommLSCheckStatus // Status structure
  lsrArgs TCommLSRead         // Read structure
  Value byte 0x0f // Lower nibble must be F for read
dseg ends
thread main
// Initialize variables
   mov lswArgs.Port, I2CPort
```

```
   mov lsrArgs.Port, I2CPort
   mov lscsArgs.Port, I2CPort
   set lsrArgs.BufferLen, 1  // Read 1 byte
// Initialize input port to I2C
   SetSensorType(I2CPort,IN_TYPE_LOWSPEED)
   SetSensorMode(I2CPort,IN_MODE_RAW)
   ResetSensor(I2CPort)
Loop:  // Top of loop
// Build buffer and write port
   arrbuild lswArgs.Buffer, I2CAddress, Value
   set lswArgs.ReturnLen, 1 // Read back 1 byte
   syscall CommLSWrite, lswArgs
Wait: // Wait till done
   syscall CommLSCheckStatus, lscsArgs
   brtst GT, Wait, lscsArgs.Result
// Read port
   syscall CommLSRead, lsrArgs
// Move lower nibble to top
   index Value, lsrArgs.Buffer, 0
   mul Value, Value, 16
// Make sure lower nibble is F
   or Value, Value, 0x0f
// Start over
   jmp Loop
endt
```

Simon Game

Simon is a deceptively simple game in which the computer generates an ever-lengthening sequence of random flashing lights that you try to reproduce from memory. Moving the Four Ins and Outs circuit to a PCB makes the game look more professional. Figure 13-12 shows how the circuit was built on a breadboard. This happens to be flipped around the right end of the board because the other end had already been used for a different project. The complete listing of the Simon NBC program is in Appendix C.

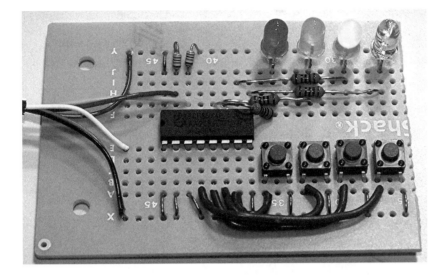

Figure 13-12. *Simon game*

Relay Outputs

We doubt that you only want to blink LEDs and play games with your I²C bus. Making the outputs useful requires adding circuitry that allows higher voltages and currents than the PCF8574 can handle. One of the easiest ways is to use a relay, and you can buy reed relays—for example, Radio Shack #275-232 or Digi-Key #306-1019-ND—that operate directly off the feeble 25mA available from the output pin.

Figure 13-13 is a schematic for an I²C interface with two relay outputs. Obviously, you could control all eight outputs in the same way. As you learned in Chapter 12, diodes D1 and D2 (1N4148) are necessary to protect the PCF8574 when the relays RL1 and RL2 are turned off.

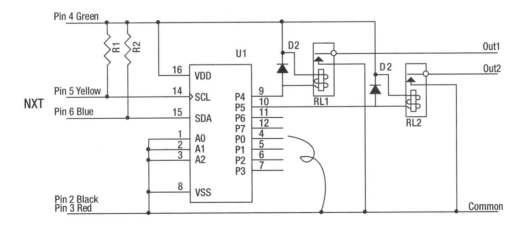

Figure 13-13. *Relay output*

The circuit is essentially the same as the previous designs, and it should be easy to figure out how to build it onto a solderless breadboard, as in Figure 13-14. The short wire lead is used to make contact temporally with pins 4 or 5 on the PCF8574 while running the Low2High program to test the relay operation. Finally, Figure 13-15 shows how to use one of the relays in the project to control an old RCX-style motor from a LEGO battery box.

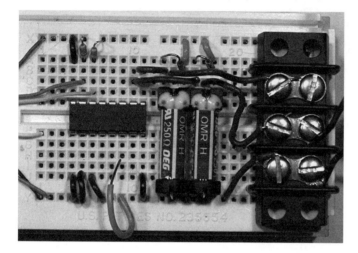

Figure 13-14. *Relay output on solderless breadboard*

Figure 13-15. *Relay output controlling an RCX-style motor*

PCF8591

Another useful I²C integrated circuit is the PCF8591 8-bit analog-to-digital (A/D) converter. It has four channels of analog input and a single channel of analog output. You can see the basic functionality of the part in Figure 13-16. You make the 8-bit A/D by comparing the output of the digital-to-analog (D/A) converter to the selected analog input. A process called *successive approximation* determines the correct value in just eight clock cycles. The digital results range from 0 to 255, and if you multiply the result by 4, it will look like the Raw values from the NXT A/D.

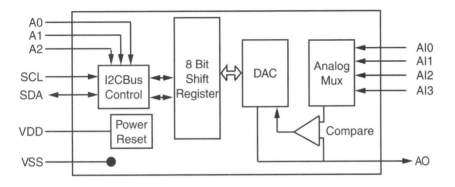

Figure 13-16. *PCF8591 8-bit A/D and D/A*

Each PCF8591 has three address lines that allow you to put up to eight of them on a single I²C bus. With all address lines tied to VSS, the base address is 90 hexadecimal (0x90), and you can use Figure 13-17 to derive the other address values.

1	0	0	1	A2	A1	A0	0

PCF8591   Address

Figure 13-17. *PCF8591 addressing*

The PCF8591 has several options that are configured by writing a control byte to it. Figure 13-18 is a diagram of the control byte. The product data sheet explains the control in more detail, but for now all we care about is setting the Auto Increment bit to one. That means the conversions will start with channel 0 and automatically increment to the next channel for every byte that is read from the part.

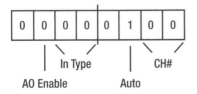

Figure 13-18. *Control byte*

Programming for the part only requires writing the control byte and then reading five bytes back. The first byte back is actually an old conversion value and should be ignored. The last four bytes are the new values for channels 0 through 3. Although you could read the part one channel at a time, reading all four is just as easy.

Four Analog Ins

Figure 13-19 shows a circuit that can read four analog inputs. Channels 0 and 1 have 10kΩ pull-up resistors, and you could use any of the sensors from Chapters 4, 5, 6, and 8 with them. These sensors would connect between either CH0 or CH1 and GND. Channels 2 and 3 have potentiometers connected, but unlike the pots in Chapter 6, they read a voltage linearly related to the shaft angle. That's because they're voltage dividers for the full power supply voltage, not just a divider with the 10kΩ pull-up inside the NXT.

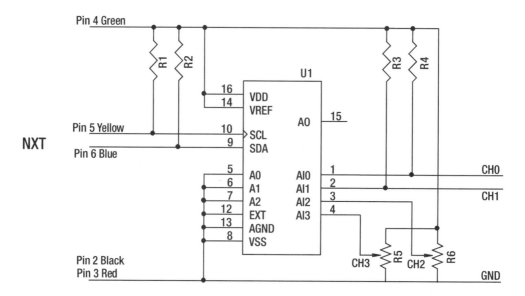

Figure 13-19. *Four Analog Ins circuit*

The bill of materials is in Table 13-5 and the step-by-step instructions are in Table 13-6. Refer to Figure 13-20 for the complete construction of the Four Analog Ins on a solderless breadboard. Although the potentiometers are shown attached directly to the breadboard, most likely they would be connected on long wires to measure the angle of a joint some distance from the circuit.

Table 13-5. *Four Analog Ins Bill of Materials*

Component	Part Number	Description	Digi-Key
U1	PCF8591	I²C Quad Analog Input	568-1087-5-ND
R1 and R2	82kΩ	1/4 W 1% Film Resistors	P82.0KCACT-ND
R3 and R4	10kΩ	1/4 W 1% Film Resistors	P10.0KCACT-ND
R5 and R6	10kΩ	Potentiometers	3310C-001-103-ND

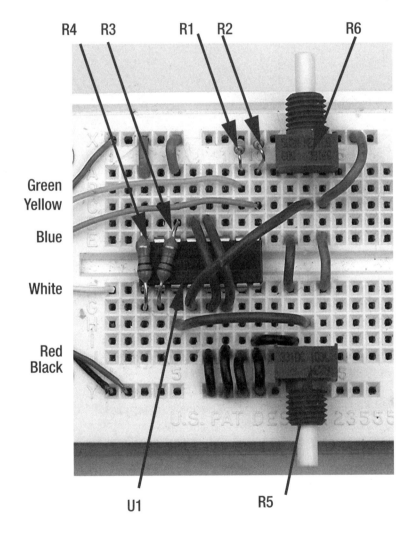

Figure 13-20. *Four Analog Ins on solderless breadboard*

Table 13-6. *Four Analog Ins Component Placement*

Component	Start	End
U1 pin 1	F3	
R1	X9	A9
R2	X10	A10
R3	D5	G4
R4	D3	G3
R5 left center right	J12	J14
R6 left center right	A14	A12
J1	X3	A3
J2	X5	A5
J3	D6	G7
J4	D7	G8
J5	J7	Y7
J6	J8	Y8
J7	J9	Y9
J8	J10	Y10
J9	I10	I12
J10	F12	E12
J11	F14	E14
J12	C14	X16
J13	C13	G6
J14	H5	H13
NXT Green White	X1	H1
NXT Red Black	Y2	Y1
NXT Blue Yellow	C10	B9

A subroutine to read all four channels of the PCF8591 is shown in Listing 13-4, with the complete test program listing in Appendix C. A structure named atod has four one-byte elements—ch0 to ch3—that receive the converter values. The system call to CommLSWrite starts the transmission, and you must wait in a loop till the status shows that the operation is complete. In case something goes wrong and there aren't five bytes in the receive buffer, you try to restart the process with another write. You could multiply the values by four and they would look like the NXT Raw values.

Listing 13-4. *Atod4 NBC Subroutine*

```
subroutine Atod4
Atod4top:
    syscall CommLSWrite, lswArgs
Atod4Wait:
    syscall CommLSCheckStatus, lscsArgs
```

```
      brtst GT, Atod4Wait, lscsArgs.Result
      brcmp NEQ, Atod4top, lscsArgs.BytesReady, 5
      syscall CommLSRead, lsrArgs
      index atod.ch0, lsrArgs.Buffer, 1
      index atod.ch1, lsrArgs.Buffer, 2
      index atod.ch2, lsrArgs.Buffer, 3
      index atod.ch3, lsrArgs.Buffer, 4
      return
ends
```

Without anything connected, channels 0 and 1 will read 255. You need to customize this design for your particular needs. You might want all potentiometer inputs, or you might want to connect it to four passive-style sensors. In Chapter 14 we'll show you how to combine the Four Analog Ins with a graphics program to make a Pong video game.

Color Sensor

You can use an NXT sensor port as both an I²C interface and as a passive sensor input at the same time. You'll put that feature to good use by building a reflective light Color Sensor. LEDs are used to flood an object with light at each of three colors: red, green, and blue. The amount of reflected light at each color is measured with our old friend from Chapter 5, the CdS Light Dependent Resistor (LDR). It's an excellent sensor for this job because it can be easily read by the NXT input and has a spectral sensitivity close to human vision. Figure 13-21 shows the cluster of three LEDs surrounding the LDR, and how heat shrink tubing has been fitted around them to keep their light from directly hitting the LDR.

Figure 13-21. *LEDs and LDR for Color Sensor*

The Color Sensor schematic is shown in Figure 13-22. Values for R3, R4, and R5 are carefully selected to make the LEDs produce a balanced amount of light, and you might need to adjust their values for your particular LEDs. Use the brightest LEDs you can get and a "pure green" green LED if possible. You can even use a tri-color LED if you can find one with a common anode and in a package you like. The resistors are adjusted by calibrating the sensor to a white object and making all three colors read the same value. Table 13-7 has the complete bill of materials.

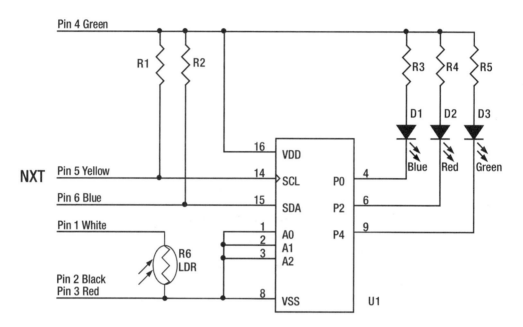

Figure 13-22. *Color Sensor schematic*

Table 13-7. *Color Sensor Bill of Materials*

Component	Part Number	Description	Digi-Key
U1	PCF8574	I²C Digital Port	296-13109-5-ND
R1 and R2	82kΩ	1/4 W 1% Film Resistors	P82.0KCACT-ND
R3	390Ω	1/4 W 1% Film Resistor	P390CACT-ND
R4	100Ω	1/4 W 1% Film Resistor	P100CACT-ND
R5	820Ω	1/4 W 1% Film Resistor	P820CACT-ND
R6	CdS LDR	CdS Photoresistor	PDV-P8001-ND
D1	Blue LED		160-1610-ND
D2	Red LED		160-1499-ND
D3	Green LED		160-1615-ND

Listing 13-5 is the subroutine from the Color Sensor program that deals with the hardware. You can find the full listing in Appendix C. It's called three times—once for each LED—to get the reflected light values that will be used to compute the hue. You select the particular LED by setting the value of variable Led to 1, 4, or 0x10. Notice the LEDs are turned off at the end, which helps the CdS sensor sensitivity and protects your eyes from the bright light.

Listing 13-5. *ReadColorComponent Subroutine of Color Sensor*

```
// input Led (1,4,0x10) -> led to light
// output Light -> reflected light level
subroutine ReadColorComponent
    xor Value, Led, 0xff
    arrbuild lswArgs.Buffer, I2CAddress, Value
    syscall CommLSWrite, lswArgs
Wait1: // Wait till done
    syscall CommLSCheckStatus, lscsArgs
    brtst GT, Wait1, lscsArgs.Result
    wait 20
    ReadSensor(I2CPort,Light)
    sub Light, 1024, Light

    arrbuild lswArgs.Buffer, I2CAddress, 0xff
    syscall CommLSWrite, lswArgs
Wait2: // Wait till done
    syscall CommLSCheckStatus, lscsArgs
    brtst GT, Wait2, lscsArgs.Result
    wait 10
    return
ends
```

Construction on the solderless breadboard is straightforward, as shown in Figure 13-23. Start with step-by-step assembly instructions from the Eight Outs project in Table 13-2 until you get to R3, then start following the instructions in Table 13-8. The sensor can be left on the solderless breadboard and mounted as in Figure 13-24 to make the finished Color Sensor. You might notice that this breadboard layout is different from the one you just developed, but it works exactly the same way.

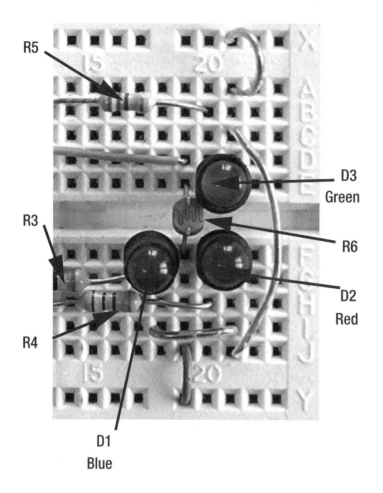

Figure 13-23. *Color Sensor on solderless breadboard*

Table 13-8. *Color Sensor Component Placement*

Component	Start	End
R3	G7	G17
R4	H9	H20
R5	B20	B10
R6	E19	F19
D1 anode cathode	F18	F17
D2 anode cathode	F21	F20
D3 anode cathode	E21	E20
J6	D19	G1
J7	Y19	J19
J8	I18	I21
J9	J21	C21
J10	X21	A21

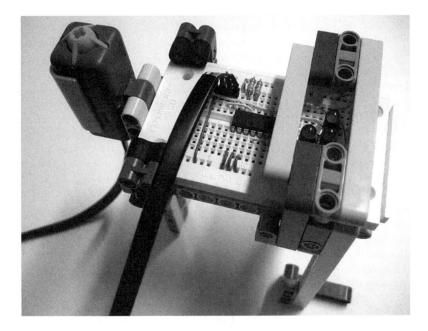

Figure 13-24. *Finished Color Sensor*

You can program this sensor and the T-56 robot arm to sort bricks by color into separate bins. The bricks are actually small blocks made from four 2 by 8 stud blocks. Figure 13-25 shows the finished robot, and the RobotC control program for it is listed in Appendix C. You need to modify the T-56 gripper to make picking up bricks easier; you can see a close-up of it in Figure 13-26.

Figure 13-25. *T-56 robot sorting colored bricks*

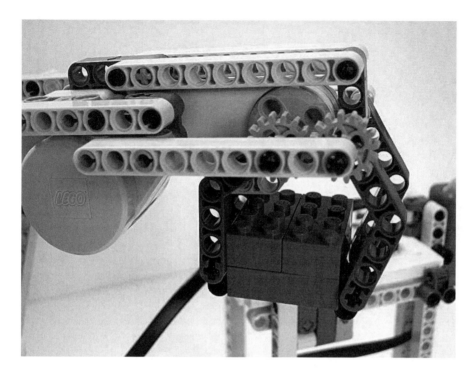

Figure 13-26. *Close-up of modified T-56 gripper*

An alternative to the CdS LDR is the TSL2550 ambient light sensor with an integrated I²C bus interface. Figure 13-27 shows how the part can be added to the PCF8574 I²C bus without any additional resistors. The small capacitor is necessary for power supply filtering. The part is in a small surface-mount package that requires a little adapter (see Figure 13-28) to use it with the solderless breadboard. A program to use this alternative part is also listed in Appendix C. Notice that the TSL2550 I²C address is 0x72.

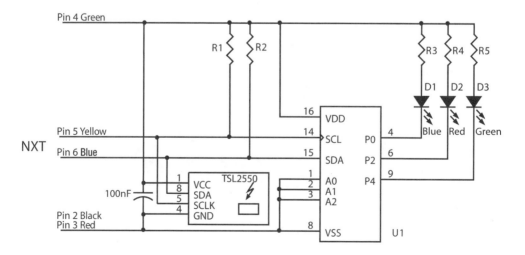

Figure 13-27. *Color Sensor using TSL2550*

Figure 13-28. *TSL2550 soldered to DIP socket adapter*

Going Further

We have just scratched the surface of I²C expansion. Integrated circuits are available that have real-time clocks, memory, and other interesting functions. You can even use the bus to interconnect with other computers. For example, the LEGO Ultrasonic Sensor has its own processor and communicates through the I²C bus to the NXT. Third-party suppliers provide compasses, accelerometers, and other sophisticated sensors that would be impossible without the functionality available from the I²C bus.

CHAPTER 14

■ ■ ■

Cool Combinations

In this chapter we'll investigate some examples of the cool things you can do with NXT when it's combined with other software and hardware.

Data Logging

Some experiments take a long time to perform, and waiting around for hours to write down the data every few minutes can be mind numbing, to say the least. Fortunately, the NXT can automatically log data into a file. You can store the numbers in the file in a text format that spreadsheet programs can import. Once the data is in a spreadsheet, you can process and plot it to produce graphs for a lab report.

Figure 14-1 is a basic data-logging program written in NXT-G. It should be easy to modify it for your particular application. Notice you must include the Keep Alive block or the NXT will fall asleep during your experiment and ruin everything. You put data into a file whose name is set in the File Access block menu shown in Figure 14-2. It's also important to close the data file when the program is done, and that's what the final File Access block is doing.

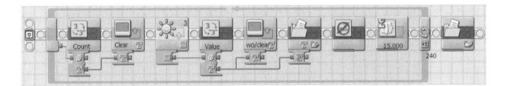

Figure 14-1. *Light level data logging program*

Figure 14-2. *File Access menu*

The Wait block at the end of the loop sets the time between samples—in this case, 15 seconds. The number of samples is set by the "Until" in the loop count menu shown in Figure 14-3. If the loop count is set to 240 and the time between samples is 15s, then the total data logging time is 3,600 seconds or one hour. When you're first trying data logging, you might want to set the Wait to a few seconds and only take a few samples to make sure everything is working correctly. The sensor in this experiment is set for Light. You might use the other sensors to log Temperature, Sound level, or Distance. The first data point is taken when you start the program, so you need to have everything ready at the start.

Control:	Count	▾
Until:	Count:	240
Show:	☑ ▪▪ Counter	

Figure 14-3. *Loop menu*

Every time you run the program, you need to go into the NXT-G environment to retrieve the data file. First, click the NXT window button (see Figure 14-4). Then, select the Memory tab (see Figure 14-5), and on the Memory page, click the Other file type (see Figure 14-6). Select the appropriate data file name and click the Upload button. Save the file somewhere on your computer where you can feed it to your spreadsheet program. Remember to delete the file from the NXT, or the next time you run the program it will just add the new data to the end of the old file.

NXT window

Figure 14-4. *NXT window button*

Communications	Memory				NXT Data	
					Your current NXT is:	
Name		Connection Type	Status	▲	Name:	NXT
◉ NXT		USB	Connected		Battery:	9.2
					Connection:	USB
					Free Storage:	62.5 KB
				▼	Firmware version:	1.03
Connect	Remove			Scan	Close	

Figure 14-5. *Select the Memory tab*

Figure 14-6. *Memory tab*

You're probably familiar with the handheld light sticks used for emergency flashlights. They also make a tiny version of these for fishing. The smaller light stick is easier to enclose in a box made out of LEGO bricks, as in Figure 14-7. Seal around the Light Sensor with black electrical tape to make sure no stray light bothers the experiment.

Figure 14-7. *Black box to hold the light stick*

When you're ready, break the little vial inside the glow stick to energize it, put it in the box, put the lid on, start the program, and come back in an hour. Retrieve the data file and open it with a text-based editor such as Notepad. You can see the first few lines of the data file in Figure 14-8. In the Edit pull-down menu, pick Select All and then Copy.

Figure 14-8. *DataFile opened with Notepad*

Open your spreadsheet program and select cell A1. Then in the Edit pull-down menu, choose Paste. All the data numbers should fill the A column, as shown in Figure 14-9. Next, in the Tools pull-down menu, select Chart, or follow whatever procedure generates plots for your particular program. A wizard, like the one shown in Figure 14-10, allows customization of the chart for your particular experimental data.

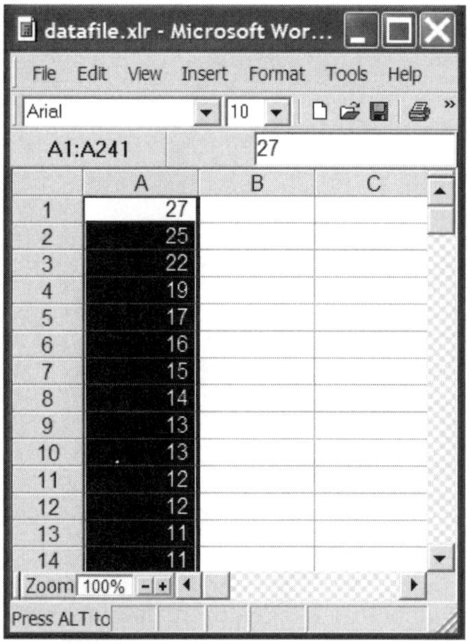

Figure 14-9. *Data pasted into the spreadsheet*

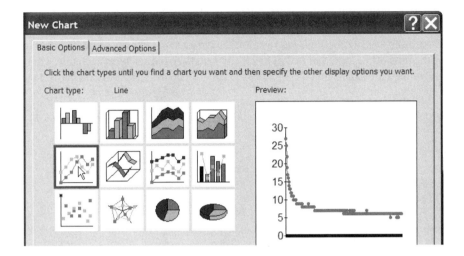

Figure 14-10. *Data plotted in the spreadsheet*

As you can see in the finished plot shown in Figure 14-11, the brightness of the light quickly drops and then stabilizes. You could make this into more of a science project by making multiple runs with sticks that are at different temperatures.

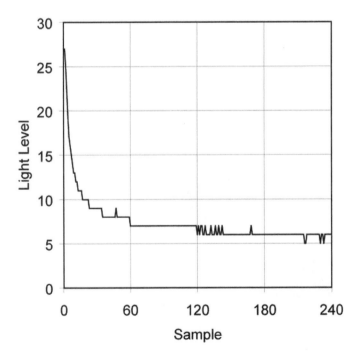

Figure 14-11. *Light level over time*

Another interesting long-term experiment would be to observe the temperature of a disposable hand warmer over time (see Figure 14-12) using the Temperature Sensor from Chapter 5. These devices work by an exothermic chemical reaction that creates rust. There's some iron dust in the bag along with some other ingredients that cause the iron to rust quickly and heat up when it's exposed to moisture in the air. It can take ten hours to fully use up the supply of iron in the bag.

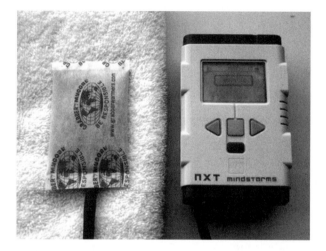

Figure 14-12. *Data logging the temperature of a hand warmer*

NXT-to-NXT Bluetooth Remote Control

For this project you'll combine two NXTs. An NXT can communicate with another NXT using a wireless technology called Bluetooth. One NXT has the back-mounted joystick from Chapter 6 and is running a program called bluesend. The other is the NXT Quick Start vehicle running a program called bluereceive. Figure 14-13 shows the pair ready for action.

Figure 14-13. *Joystick remote control and Quick Start vehicle*

When the bluesend program starts, the joystick should be in the centered position. The Raw values for the two pots are recorded as Pzero for the power and Szero for the steering, as shown in Figure 14-14. Whenever the joystick is returned to the starting position, the vehicle will be going straight but at zero speed.

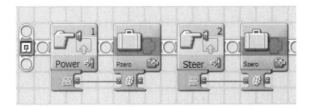

Figure 14-14. *Remote-control bluesend program initialization*

Figure 14-15 is the main loop of the bluesend program, which reads each of the joystick pots and subtracts the initial positions. The values tend to be too large for the Motor block in the vehicle so they're divided by five. These two values are sent to Bluetooth connection 1 and mailboxes 1 and 2. It's up to the remote-control vehicle to receive these values and convert them into speed and steering commands.

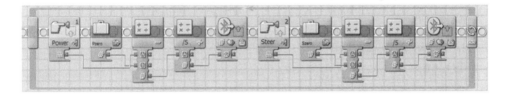

Figure 14-15. *Remote-control bluesend program main loop*

The NXT Quick Start vehicle is a convenient starting point for a remote-control vehicle. All you need to do is load the bluereceive program shown in Figure 14-16. The receiver program just gets the steering and power values for a Move block from the two Bluetooth mailboxes. You determine the direction of the power command by comparing it to zero.

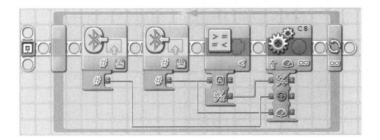

Figure 14-16. *Remote-control bluereceive program*

You need to use the Bluetooth menu on the remote-control NXT to establish the connection with the vehicle NXT as connection 1, and then run the programs. Refer to the LEGO MINDSTORMS User Guide chapter on Bluetooth for detailed instructions on establishing links between NXTs. It can be tricky and might require several tries to establish a connection.

LEGO Train Station

The NXT is a natural for automating LEGO train control. The variable output power from the NXT is sufficient to operate a train motor, and you can use the Light Sensor to detect the presence of the train. The power to the tracks uses the same connector as the old RCX (see Figure 14-17). That means you can connect the NXT with the same conversion cable (LEGO #8528) used for the RCX sensors or motor. The prolonged power consumption of operating trains will probably make you wish you had the NXT rechargeable battery pack (LEGO #9798).

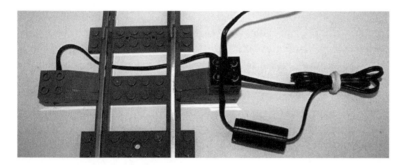

Figure 14-17. *Track electrical connections*

The LEGO train track ties have two rows of regular LEGO studs that you can use to mount the sensor using plates, as can be seen in Figure 14-18. You must set the sensor back far enough to avoid being hit by the train as it goes by, but close enough for the reflected light from the train car to be registered by the NXT.

Figure 14-18. *Light Sensor as a train detector*

An NXT-G program to control a train station is shown in Figure 14-19. The train automatically stops at the station long enough to pick up passengers and then pulls away. Power is supplied to the train motor till the Light Sensor detects the reflection from the locomotive. It then cuts the power to make the engine stop. It waits one second at the station and then pulls away. The on time in the last motor block guarantees that the train will be clear of the station before the program loops back to the beginning. If the train was on a circular track, it would stop every time it came around to the station.

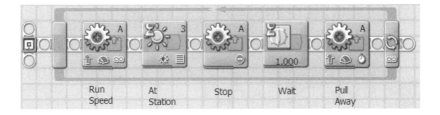

Figure 14-19. *Train station control program*

Panoramic Camera

The base of the RoboArm T-56 has a turntable (see Figure 14-20) that makes a great platform for rotating a camera to take panoramic photographs. The camera used in this example is a Jazz Photo JDC-11, but many other inexpensive digital cameras are available like it. You need to modify the holder and trigger design from the one shown in Figure 14-21 to suit the one you have.

Figure 14-20. *Turntable in base of RoboArm T-56*

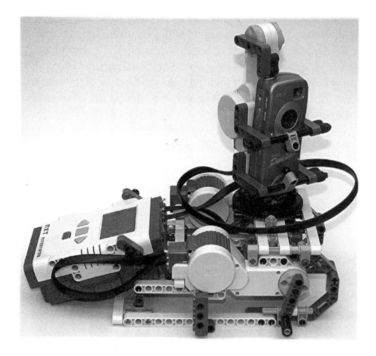

Figure 14-21. *Digital camera and trigger mounted on base*

The width of the camera field of view is 55 degrees, but it's important to allow plenty of overlap between images to make merging the photographs easier. You also want to make sure the pan is over 360 degrees to allow some cropping on the ends. The turntable is geared down so much that it takes 168 full turns of the motor for only one rotation. The worm gear only advances the 24-tooth gear by one tooth per motor revolution. The turntable has 56 teeth, so the 8-tooth gear makes 7 revolutions for 1 turntable rotation, and 7 times 24 equals 168. That works out to only 2.2 degrees per turn. If you turn the motor 16 times, then the camera will move 35 degrees, allowing plenty of overlap between shots. Repeating this 11 times will create a pan of over 380 degrees.

Pushing the camera shutter button only requires running the motor forward long enough to guarantee the arm has made good contact with it. A short reversal is necessary to make sure the button is fully released. The whole NXT-G program is shown in Figure 14-22.

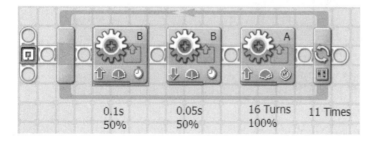

Figure 14-22. *NXT-G panoramic camera control*

You can use just about any photo editing software to merge the 11 photos into one long panorama. For example, Figures 14-23 and 14-24 show how Microsoft Photo Editor was used. The first photo in the sequence is expanded to have ten times the left margin so that the other photos can be simply cut and pasted into place. An example of a full 360-degree panorama is shown in Figure 14-25.

Figure 14-23. *Expanding the first photo's width*

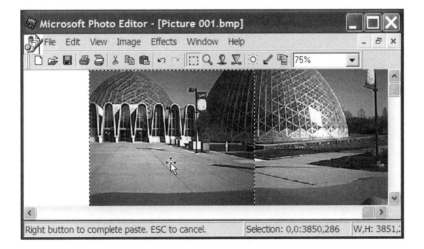

Figure 14-24. *The other photos are pasted and adjusted one at a time.*

Figure 14-25. *Finished 360-degree panoramic photo*

Graphics

A nice freeware program called nxtRICedit by Andreas Dreier lets you create and modify the graphics files used for the NXT display (see Figure 14-26). These files carry the RIC extension, and can be found in a subdirectory of the LEGO software. In fact, any RIC files in that directory will show up in the image selection list for the NXT-G Display block. Conveniently, the default directory for nxtRICedit is this folder.

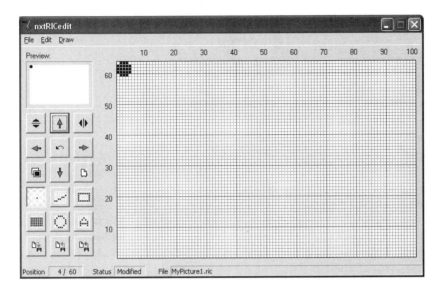

Figure 14-26. *NxtRICedit by Andreas Dreier*

In addition to creating images, the program can convert photographic images to the RIC format. The NXT display is pure black and white with no grayscale, so contrast is a critical adjustment. Figure 14-27 shows part of the Import window where the contrast can be adjusted.

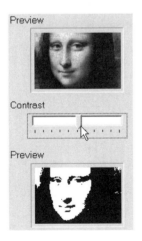

Figure 14-27. *Contrast adjustment in the Import window*

The RIC file is loaded into the NXT automatically when you load an NXT-G program that contains a Display block that uses the file. Figure 14-28 shows the selection of the file created in the preceding example. For full-screen images, you'll want to set the X and Y to 0.

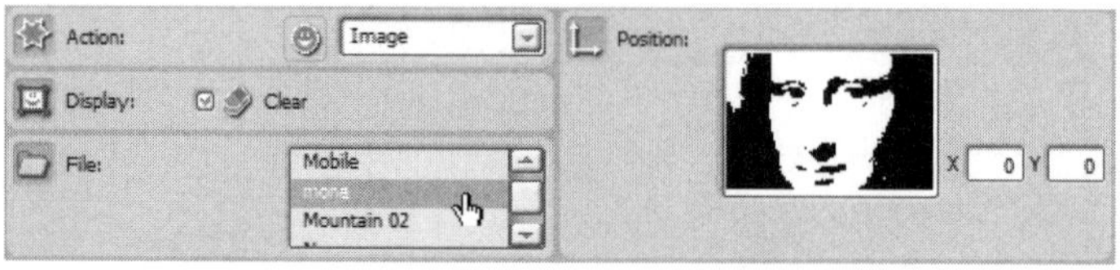

Figure 14-28. *NXT-G Display Options box*

If you're animating small images on the NXT display, you'll need to erase the old image before drawing it in its new location. You can erase the entire screen and start over, but that can be a problem if you have a lot of other graphics. The best thing to do is draw an all-white image of the same size over the original.

For example, if you're moving the little ball image shown being created in Figure 14-26, you'd draw a five-by-five pixel white block to erase it and then redraw it at its new location. You create this white block image, oddly enough, by adding borders to a blank file. This works because the program normally saves only the minimal area containing black pixels. In nxtRICedit, select File New, then Save As. In the Add Borders part of the Save window, enter a five-by-five border as shown in Figure 14-29. The program then saves a small white box.

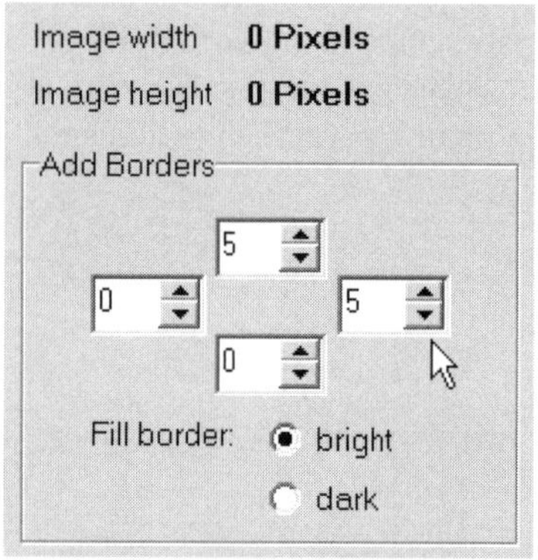

Figure 14-29. *Making a five-by-five white box RIC file*

NXT Pong Video Game

You can make a Pong video game by combining the nxtRICedit tool to create the graphic elements and the Four Analog Ins project from Chapter 13 for paddle control. Figure 14-30 shows a screen shot of the game, and you can find the complete NBC program listing in Appendix C. The position of the paddles is determined by the values from channels 2 and 3 on the analog-to-digital converter. Because the vertical screen resolution is only 60 pixels, the converter value, which can be as large as 255, must be divided by 4 to scale it down. The ball's velocity is changed by the following situations: if it has hit a paddle, bounced off the top or bottom of the screen, or gone off the ends of the field.

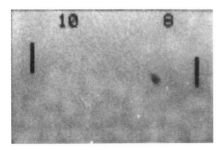

Figure 14-30. *NXT Pong screen shot*

Figure 14-31 shows the finished Pong game. The Four Analog Ins project has been moved to a PCB, and 40-tooth gears serve as the player control knobs. The board is attached to a beam with two small screws. The paddles are 2-pixel-wide and 16-pixel-tall black rectangles and need counterpart 2-by-16 white rectangles to erase them. The ball is a five-pixel square. nxtRICedit creates these four RIC files and loads them into the NXT using the NXT-G programming environment. However, the complexity of the program requires a language such as NBC.

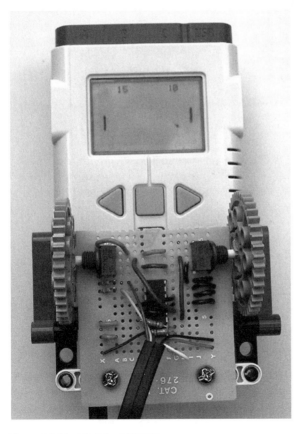

Figure 14-31. *Finished NXT Pong game*

Remotely Guided Vehicle

Inexpensive digital cameras or web cams make great attachments for making remotely guided vehicles. It's like you're riding along as you pilot your vehicle while watching the live video on the computer screen. The cameras are easily mounted to the Quick Start vehicle with a just few beams, as shown in Figure 14-32. You'll probably want to buy some USB extension cords to expand the area you can explore, but USB can't be extended much beyond 16 feet (5m) total. You could also use a wireless camera so your vehicle would be completely untethered.

Figure 14-32. *Inexpensive digital camera fitted to the vehicle*

Before you can remotely control your NXT, you need to establish a Bluetooth connection to it from the PC. Sometimes this can be tricky, so we'll go through the whole process step by step. Start by opening the Windows Control Panel and double-clicking the Bluetooth Devices icon, as shown in Figure 14-33.

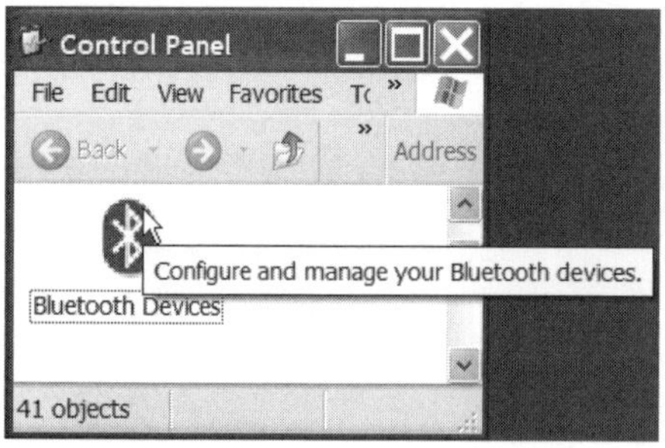

Figure 14-33. *Windows Control Panel*

A window with your known Bluetooth Devices shows up, as in Figure 14-34. If there's already an NXT device in the window, select it and click the Remove button. Don't worry, you'll reconnect to it in just a moment. When the NXT device icon is gone, click the Add button.

Figure 14-34. *Devices tab of the Bluetooth Devices window*

An Add Bluetooth Device Wizard opens, as in Figure 14-35. Make sure your NXT is turned on, then select the check mark in the wizard that says "My device is set up and ready to be found." Then click the Next> button.

Figure 14-35. *Add Bluetooth Device Wizard*

After searching, the NXT Bluetooth icon should show up, as in Figure 14-36. Double-click the icon and the passkey window opens.

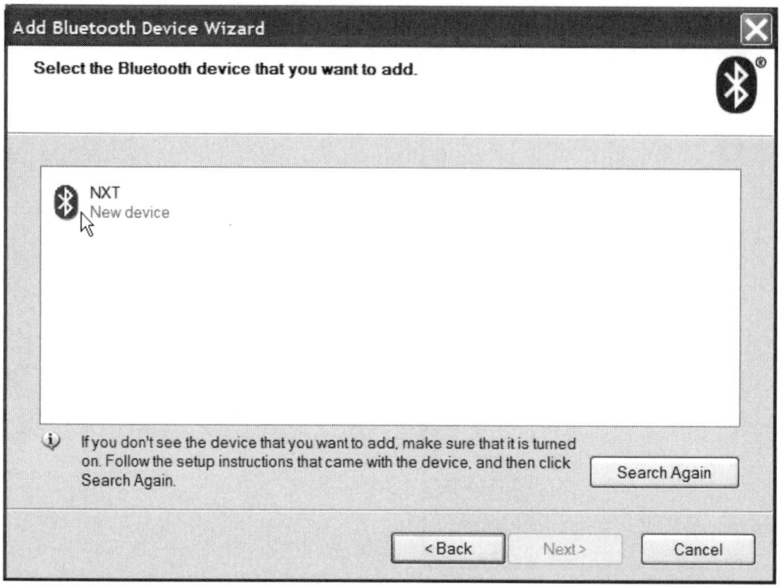

Add Bluetooth Device Wizard   ⊠

Select the Bluetooth device that you want to add.

> NXT
> New device

ⓘ If you don't see the device that you want to add, make sure that it is turned on. Follow the setup instructions that came with the device, and then click Search Again.

Search Again

< Back   Next >   Cancel

Figure 14-36. *Double-click the NXT Bluetooth Icon*

In the passkey window (see Figure 14-37) select "Let me choose my own passkey" and enter **1234**. Then select the Next> button. The NXT should make a little chirping noise and you'll need to confirm the passkey by pressing the orange button.

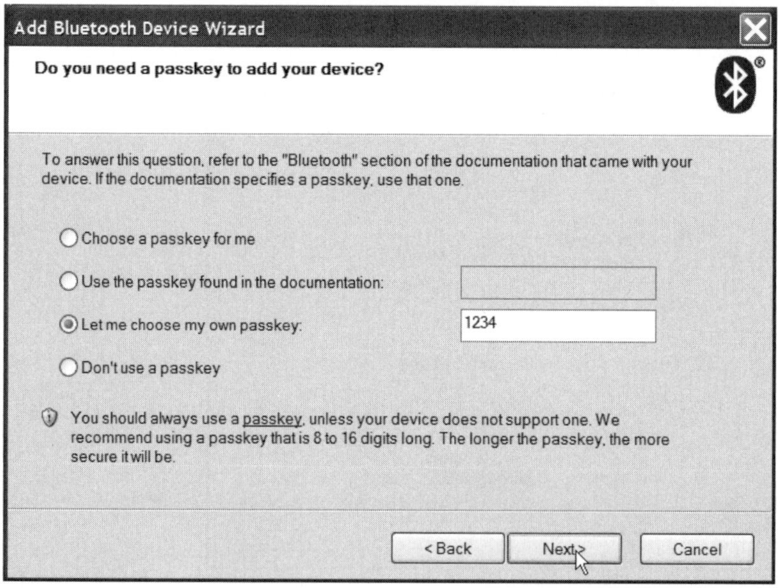

Add Bluetooth Device Wizard   ⊠

Do you need a passkey to add your device?

To answer this question, refer to the "Bluetooth" section of the documentation that came with your device. If the documentation specifies a passkey, use that one.

○ Choose a passkey for me

○ Use the passkey found in the documentation:

◉ Let me choose my own passkey: 1234

○ Don't use a passkey

ⓘ You should always use a <u>passkey</u>, unless your device does not support one. We recommend using a passkey that is 8 to 16 digits long. The longer the passkey, the more secure it will be.

< Back   Next >   Cancel

Figure 14-37. *Passkey window*

The Completing the Add Bluetooth Device Wizard window looks like Figure 14-38; it shows the COM ports that the NXT will be using. The lower number of these, COM9 in this case, will be needed by the NXT remote-control program.

Figure 14-38. *COM port information*

You can check the port numbers at any time by selecting the COM Ports tab on the Bluetooth Devices window, as in Figure 14-39. You should only need to go through this whole process once because your computer and the NXT will remember their relationship.

Figure 14-39. *COM Ports tab of the Bluetooth Devices window*

NXT-remote is a great little freeware NXT remote-control program by Anders Søborg. The first thing you need to do when you run NXT-remote is make a Bluetooth connection. Enter the correct COM number, if needed, and press the Connect button. You should see "Connection Established" in the Debug window and the NXT will beep. Next, make sure the correct motors are selected; Motor 1 is C and Motor 2 is B. Driving is simply a matter of pressing the arrow buttons in the direction you want to go. Arrange the live video window and the NXT-remote window to be side by side, as in Figure 14-40. Try driving by only looking at the video screen like a true remotely guided vehicle. When you see something interesting you can take a picture of it by pressing the Capture button.

Figure 14-40. *Live Video and NXT-remote by Anders Søborg*

Other NXT remote-control PC programs are available, most notably Dashboard Designer from RoboDNA. However, there are remote-control methods that don't use the PC. LEGO endorses a method that uses Bluetooth-enabled PDAs and mobile phones. A program called NXT Director from Razix appears to be built on this technology.

■■■

Breadboard Construction Technique

Building the more advanced projects in this book might require you to learn some new skills. Most electronic products today use construction techniques that involve parts so small you need a microscope to handle them. Fortunately, larger electrical components that you can reasonably work with are still available. Methods to build with these parts have been around for decades, and everything you need is available at Radio Shack or other electronic distributors.

Solderless Breadboard

The first tool to become familiar with is the solderless breadboard. The term *breadboard* dates back to when electronic hobbyists literally built projects on a plank of wood intended for cutting bread. Many styles of breadboards are available, but they all consist of columns of interconnected holes used for connecting components, and a few long rows of holes at the top and bottom used for connecting power.

Radio Shack sells a small breadboard (Catalog Number: 276-175) that is big enough to build all the projects in this book (see Figure A-1). A nice feature of this particular breadboard is that it has row and column identification marks that make construction easier. Throughout this book we indicate the exact row and column where you should insert the lead of a device. By following these instructions precisely, your chance of making a mistake will be greatly reduced.

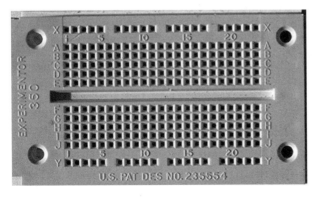

Figure A-1. *Solderless prototype breadboard*

Building on the Breadboard

We demonstrate the construction process through a simple example. Figure A-2 shows a minimal 9V powered sensor design. The design just takes care of separating the power and sensor read parts of the 9V powered interface described in Chapter 9. Nevertheless, the circuit is useful for voltage input where measured voltage is something that can't be loaded by the NXT internal 10kΩ resistor. It only has four parts, listed in the bill of materials in Table A-1.

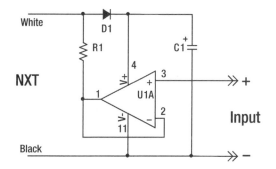

Figure A-2. *Voltage input*

Table A-1. *Bill of Materials*

Component	Part Number	Description	Radio Shack
U1	LM324	Quad OpAmp	276-1711
D1	1N4148	Small Signal Diode	276-1122
R1	1kΩ	1/4 W 5% Carbon Film Resistor	271-1321
C1	22uF	16V or higher Electrolytic Capacitor	272-1014

All the parts have been placed on the breadboard in Figure A-3. Most of the parts have long leads to start with, and you could insert them into the same holes without cutting them shorter, but you run the risk of accidentally touching the leads together, creating short circuits. Construction consists of going down row by row in Table A-2 and connecting one component at a time. The "start" column corresponds to the first listed end of the part and the "end" the last. For example, C1's start is the positive (+) lead and the end is the negative (–) lead. J1, J2, and J3 are just wire jumpers.

Figure A-3. *Components on the solderless breadboard*

Table A-2. *Component Placement*

Component	Start	End
U1 pin 1	F4	
C1 + −	Y1	X1
J1	Y7	J7
J2	X7	A7
J3	G4	G5
D1 anode cathode	J2	Y2
R1	I2	I4
NXT white black	X2	H2
Input +	H6	I6
Input −	X10	X11

After building the circuit, you'll need to make sure that it works. While running a program that configures the port as an old RCX-type Light Sensor, check that the voltage across C1 is between 9V and 6V. You can add a potentiometer, as in Figure A-4, to input a known voltage. Using a voltmeter and a program that reads the Raw sensor value, you can create a plot like Figure A-5. The lower end of the voltage range has a flat region because the LM324 cannot output a value less than about 0.6V.

Figure A-4. *Checking the circuit*

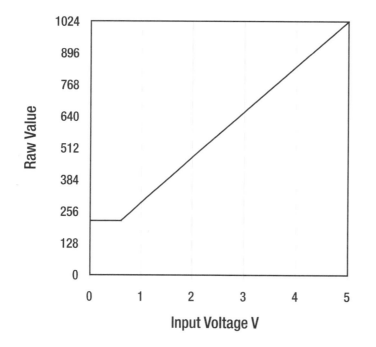

Figure A-5. *Voltage input versus Raw value plot*

You could just leave the circuit on the breadboard for as long as you needed it, but it's better to commit it permanently to a PCB. It will be more compact and much more reliable, because parts can accidentally be pulled out of the breadboard.

Printed Circuit Board

The Global Specialties Experimenter PCB or the Radio Shack 276-170 (see Figure A-6) match the layout of the electronic breadboard exactly, as can be seen in the bottom view in Figure A-7. It has the same row and column markings as the breadboard, so it should be easy to transfer the parts from the breadboard to the PCB. The only problem with the PCB is that it's way too long. That means that one Experimenter PCB could be the source for several sensors.

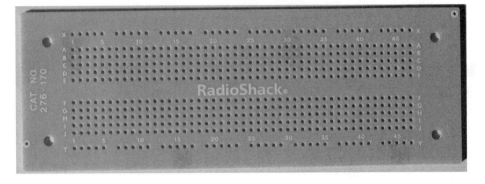

Figure A-6. *Printed circuit board that matches the solderless breadboard*

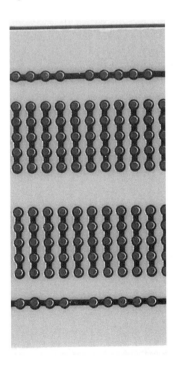

Figure A-7. *Bottom view of the PCB*

Cutting the PCB is a lot easier than you might think. All that's required is a straight-edge ruler and a sharp knife, as shown in Figure A-8. You score the board by creating a shallow groove in the top and bottom of the board along a column of holes where you want to cut the board. Once the board has been scored, it will snap by bending it at the groove.

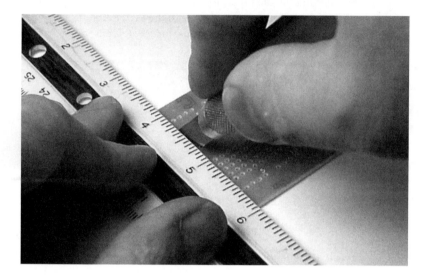

Figure A-8. *Scoring the PC board*

Start by laying the straight-edge ruler along the column of holes where you want to cut the PCB. Take a sharp knife and run it along the straight edge the entire width of the board. The knife will bump along from hole to hole. At first, don't use very much pressure. Keep running the knife along exactly the same path over and over until a groove develops. It usually takes about ten passes. Repeat the process on the bottom side of the board.

Bracing your thumbs at the groove as in Figure A-9, gently bend the board down on both sides with your fingers. It should snap with only a reasonable amount of force. If it doesn't snap, continue to cut at the grooves to make them a little deeper and try again. You'll be left with a small PCB that's just the right size for your project.

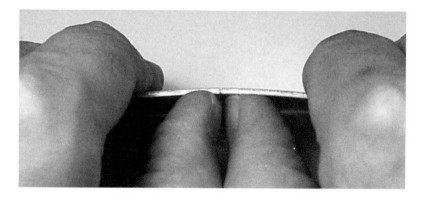

Figure A-9. *Snapping the PC board*

As you cut away other small PCBs, you'll notice that the printed column numbers won't match the solderless breadboard anymore. The original painted numbers are easily scratched off and you can remark them with permanent marker.

Soldering

Soldering the parts to the PCB is probably the scariest part. It requires a certain amount of skill, but after a few connections you'll find that it really isn't that difficult. Making good solder connections requires following a few basic rules:

- The soldering iron should be a 25-to-40 watt pencil type with a 1/8" to 3/16" chisel- or cone-shaped tip.

- Always wait at least five minutes for the soldering iron to come up to temperature.

- The solder should be rosin core 60/40 Tin-Lead content with .062" diameter. *Never* use acid core or the type used for plumbing.

■**Caution** Lead is a poison and has been proven to cause health problems, especially for young children. Never leave solder around where people may handle or eat it.

- Lead-free solder is available and works just as well, but requires a little higher melting temperature.

- When using a new tip, coat the tip with a good layer of solder and wipe off the excess with a damp sponge.

- The soldering iron must be kept clean by quickly wiping it on a damp sponge each time just before making a connection.

■**Note** Remember to unplug the soldering iron when you're done using it.

The first step in soldering a component to the PCB is making absolutely sure that you have the component leads in the right holes and that the part is oriented properly. If you have built the circuit on the breadboard first, it's a simple matter of pulling parts off the breadboard and placing them one by one. Push the leads of a component through the holes and spread the leads apart, as shown in Figure A-10, to keep the component from falling out when you turn the PCB over to solder. You can work on one part at a time, but the job will go faster if you place several parts that are close together at the same time and then solder.

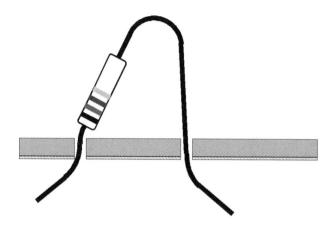

Figure A-10. *Placement of the component on a PC board*

To make a solder joint, touch the soldering iron tip to both the PCB copper pad and the component wire at the same time and allow the connection to heat for a second. Figure A-11 shows the proper placement of the soldering iron tip and the lead.

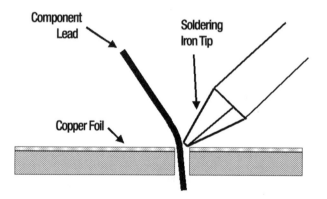

Figure A-11. *Heating the connection*

Now bring the solder to the hot connection (see Figure A-12), not the iron tip, and allow enough solder to flow around the connection, as shown in Figure A-13. You might think that the components would be instantly damaged by the high temperature of soldering. However, they're designed to tolerate it for fairly long times, and you shouldn't be afraid to take the time to make a good joint. Remove the solder and iron and then allow the connection to cool for a few seconds before moving anything. The solder should be shiny and look almost wet when it first cools.

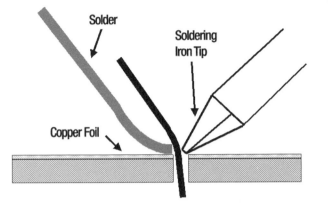

Figure A-12. *Adding solder to the connection*

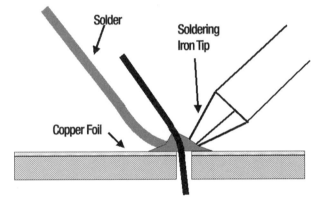

Figure A-13. *Let solder flow around the connection*

Bad solder joints, like those shown in Figure A-14, are usually the result of not heating the joint sufficiently. The joint might have voids as in the top example, or have a blob-like appearance as in the lower example. Bad joints might also look dull. Just reheat the joint and add solder if necessary.

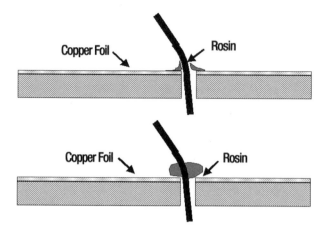

Figure A-14. *Examples of bad solder joints*

Cut off the excess component lead close to the connection with diagonal cutters. The finished joint should look like Figure A-15 in cross-section.

■**Note** Clip leads so the ends won't fly toward your eyes.

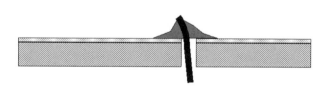

Figure A-15. *Cut excess component lead flush with the joint*

Solder bridges are a common problem when soldering this type of PCB. A little too much solder gets into the joint and flows over onto the next trace. Don't panic! Hold the PCB vertically in one hand and bring the soldering iron tip up to the bridge from below, as shown in Figure A-16. The excess solder should flow back onto the tip, where you can wipe it off on the damp sponge. Unsoldering tools are available that you can use to vacuum practically all the solder from a joint.

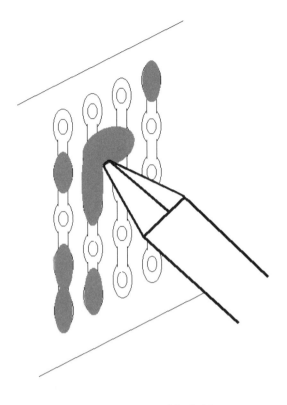

Figure A-16. *How to remove a solder bridge*

Another problem is solder covering a hole where you need to insert a part. Usually a technique similar to the bridge removal will work to clear the hole. Just coax the solder down the copper track away from the blocked hole with the soldering iron. You can also melt the solder while pushing the component lead into the hole. Because all the holes in a column are connected anyway, you can substitute placing a part into a nearby hole that isn't blocked. There's also a product called *unsoldering braid* that, when heated along with the solder, will wick up extra solder.

Building a Printed Circuit Board

Figure A-17 is what the voltage input should look like after it has been moved to a PCB. The bottom view is in Figure A-18, and you might notice that the unused pins of the LM324 haven't been soldered at all. You may solder these pins if you want, but the step is unnecessary and you are more likely to create solder bridges.

Figure A-17. *Top side of the finished voltage input*

Figure A-18. *Bottom side of the finished voltage input*

■ ■ ■

References, Links, and Sources

This appendix provides links to go beyond the information presented in the book. The links are categorized by chapter, with an additional "General Interest" category. Some of the links are to the websites of manufactures of electronic parts, and others are to companies that sell them. The book website at `http://www.apress.com` will maintain an updated list of links.

General Interest

Digi-Key: `http://www.digikey.com/`

LEGO MINDSTORMS: `http://mindstorms.lego.com/`

LEGO page with NXT Developer Kits: `http://mindstorms.lego.com/Overview/NXTreme.aspx`

Nxtbot.com blog: `http://www.NXTBot.com`

The NXT STEP blog: `http://www.thenxtstep.blogspot.com`

Nxtasy.org NXT news: `http://www.nxtasy.org/`

MINDSTORMS-related newsgroup: `http://news.lugnet.com/robotics/`

Michael Gasperi's LEGO page: `http://www.extremenxt.com/lego.htm`

Matthias Paul Scholz's NXT Tools page: `http://mynxt.matthiaspaulscholz.eu/tools/index.html`

Philippe (Philo's) LEGO page: `http://www.philohome.com/`

Radio Shack: `http://www.radioshack.com/`

SensorWiki.org: `http://sensorwiki.org/index.php/Main_Page`

Chapter 1

LEGO MINDSTORMS: http://mindstorms.lego.com/

Mindell, David, et al. "LEGO Mindstorms, The Structure of an Engineering (R)evolution": http://web.mit.edu/6.933/www/Fall2000/LegoMindstorms.pdf

Papert, Seymour. *Mindstorms: Children, Computers, and Powerful Ideas.* New York: Basic Books, 1993.

Koerner, Brendan I. "Geeks in Toyland." *Wired Magazine,* February 2006: http://www.wired.com/wired/archive/14.02/lego.html

MIT MindFest: http://www.media.mit.edu/mindfest/

Russell Nelson's LEGO MINDSTORMS Internals website: http://www.crynwr.com/lego-robotics/

Chapter 2

LEGO page with NXT Developer Kits: http://mindstorms.lego.com/Overview/NXTreme.aspx

Human vision information: http://www.onr.navy.mil/sci_tech/31/312/ncsr/devices/led/ch_11_human_vision.pdf

Homebrew Sound Sensor: http://www.extremenxt.com/sound.htm

Comparison of LEGO motors: http://www.philohome.com/motors/motorcomp.htm

Next Byte Codes: http://bricxcc.sourceforge.net/nbc/

Bricx Command Center: http://bricxcc.sourceforge.net/

RobotC: http://www-education.rec.ri.cmu.edu/robotc/index.html

Chapter 3

LEGO page with NXT Developer Kits: http://mindstorms.lego.com/Overview/NXTreme.aspx

LEGO Education: http://www.legoeducation.com/store/

Chapter 5

LEGO Store: http://shop.lego.com/

LEGO Education: http://www.legoeducation.com/store/

GE Infrastructure Sensing: http://www.thermometrics.com/

Human comfort zone: http://www.p2pays.org/ref/08/07692.pdf

The Rotronic Humidity Handbook: `http://www.rotronic-usa.com/Ref/Rotronic%20Humidity%20Handbook.pdf`

Cadmium sulfide photoresistors: `http://www.selcoproducts.com/CFM/photocell_toc.cfm`

Theremin: `http://www.thereminworld.com/`

Braitenberg Vehicles: `http://people.cs.uchicago.edu/~wiseman/vehicles/`

Braitenberg, Valentino. *Vehicles: Experiments in Synthetic Psychology*. Cambridge, MA: The MIT Press, 1986.

Chapter 6

Bourns: `http://www.bourns.com/`

LEGO Shop at Home: `http://shop.lego.com/`

Inverted pendulum: `http://en.wikipedia.org/wiki/Inverted_pendulum`

Chapter 8

DN6849SE datasheet: `http://www.ortodoxism.ro/datasheets/panasonic/SPC00004CEB.pdf`

2N3906 datasheet: `http://www.fairchildsemi.com/ds/2N/2N3906.pdf`

Acroname: `http://www.acroname.com/`

Sharp GP2D12 datasheet: `http://document.sharpsma.com/files/GP2D12-DATA-SHEET.PDF`

Sundials: `http://en.wikipedia.org/wiki/Sundial`

Chapter 9

LM324 datasheet: `http://www.national.com/ds.cgi/LM/LM124.pdf`

1N4148 datasheet: `http://www.fairchildsemi.com/ds/1N/1N4148.pdf`

Next Byte Codes: `http://bricxcc.sourceforge.net/nbc/`

Lamp filament resistance: `http://www.ee.bgu.ac.il/~pel/pdf-files/conf104.pdf`

More on filament resistance: `http://www.df.uba.ar/users/sgil/physics_paper_doc/papers_phys/e&m/light_bulb_thermom.pdf`

1230-030D-3L datasheet: `http://www.meas-spec.com/myMeas/download/pdf/english/icsensors/pressure/pcb_mountable/model_1230_ultrastable.pdf`

Chapter 10

HiTechnic: http://www.hitechnic.com/

Mindsensors.com: http://www.mindsensors.com/

Techno-stuff: http://www.techno-stuff.com/

Vernier: http://www.vernier.com/

DCP Microdevelopments: http://www.dcpmicro.com/

LEGO Education: http://www.legoeducation.com/store/

Chapter 11

The Clapper: http://www.chia.com/clapper.html

Etch A Sketch: http://www.etch-a-sketch.com/

Chapter 12

Jameco Robotic Store: http://www.robotstore.com/

Jameco Electronics: http://www.jameco.com/

Dyanalloy and Flexinol: http://www.dynalloy.com/

Potter and Brumfield: http://relays.tycoelectronics.com/pnb.asp

Globe pencil sharpener: http://www.rinovelty.com/
ProductDetail.asp?code=ST-SHGLO&sub=SRSH

1N400X datasheet: http://www.diodes.com/datasheets/ds28002.pdf

IRF510 datasheet: http://www.irf.com/product-info/datasheets/data/irf510.pdf

IRF9530 datasheet: http://www.irf.com/product-info/datasheets/data/irf530.pdf

IRF520 datasheet: http://www.irf.com/product-info/datasheets/data/irf520.pdf

STTH2R06RL datasheet: http://www.st.com/stonline/products/literature/ds/10757/
stth2r06.pdf

PS2501-4 datasheet: http://www.cel.com/pdf/datasheets/ps2501.pdf

Chapter 13

I²C manual: http://www.nxp.com/acrobat_download/applicationnotes/AN10216_1.pdf

Simon game: http://www.hasbro.com/default.cfm?page=browse&brand=660

PCF8574 and PCF8574A datasheet: http://www.cel.com/pdf/datasheets/ps2501.pdf

PCF8591 datasheet: http://www.nxp.com/acrobat_download/datasheets/PCF8591_6.pdf

Tact switch datasheet: http://www.e-switch.com/pdf/SeriesTL1105Tact.pdf

Reed Relays: http://www.cotorelay.com/html/reed_relay_8l_series.htm

Cadmium sulfide photoresistors: http://www.selcoproducts.com/CFM/photocell_toc.cfm

TSL2550 datasheet: http://www.taosinc.com/images/product/document/tsl2550-e67.pdf

Chapter 14

Jazz DigiStix camera: http://www.amazon.com/Jazz-JDC11-DigiStix-Digital-Camera/dp/B00006F2O7

Light sticks: http://science.howstuffworks.com/light-stick.htm

Hand warmers: http://www.warmers.com/

LEGO Shop at Home: http://shop.lego.com/

Panoramic photography: http://www.shortcourses.com/how/panoramic/panoramic.htm

NxtRICedit download: http://www.matthias-paul-scholz.homepage.t-online.de/lego/nxt/tools/NXTRICedit/nxtRICedit.zip

Pong: http://www.pong-story.com/

NXT-remote: http://www.norgesgade14.dk/legoSider/mindstorm_en.html

LEGO NXT Mobile Application: http://mindstorms.lego.com/Overview/Mobile%20Application.aspx

Razix and NXT Director: http://www.razix.com/nxtdirector.htm

RoboDNA and Dashboard Designer: http://robodna.com/roboDNA/

Appendix A

Global Specialties: http://www.globalspecialties.com/

1N4148 datasheet: http://www.fairchildsemi.com/ds/1N/1N4148.pdf

LM324 datasheet: http://www.national.com/ds.cgi/LM/LM124.pdf

APPENDIX C

∎∎∎

Code Listings

Arranged by chapter, here are the complete listings of the programs. You can also download them from the book website, in the Source Code/Download area at http://www.apress.com.

Chapter 9

Listing C-1. *rawmeter.nbc*

```
//------------------Variable Declarations------------------
dseg segment
      TLocation     struct
      X             sword
      Y             sword
  TLocation  ends
  TDrawText  struct
    Result   sbyte
    Location TLocation
    Text       byte[]
    Options  dword
  TDrawText    ends

  dtArgs TDrawText

  thePort byte IN_1 // sensor port 1
  theSensorType byte IN_TYPE_REFLECTION  //RCX style light
  theSensorMode byte IN_MODE_RAW  // raw data mode
  RVal sword

  SVal sword 0
  isInvalid byte
  thenTick dword
  nowTick dword

dseg ends
```

```
//-----------------Program Code-------------------------
thread main

 set dtArgs.Location.X, 40
 set dtArgs.Location.Y, 30
 set dtArgs.Options, 1        // clear screen

 setin theSensorType, thePort, Type      // write sensor type to port
 setin theSensorMode, thePort, InputMode // write sensor mode to port
 set   isInvalid, TRUE  // invalidate the sensor
 // sensor reset sequence
 setin isInvalid, thePort, InvalidData
stillInvalid:   // loop until it is not invalid
 getin isInvalid, thePort, InvalidData
 brtst NEQ, stillInvalid, isInvalid
setin  SVal, thePort, ScaledValue // reset the scaled value

Forever:
 getin  RVal, thePort, RawValue  // read in new value
 numtostr dtArgs.Text, RVal  // convert number to string
 syscall DrawText, dtArgs     // display number
 gettick nowTick  // what time is it now?
 add  thenTick, nowTick, 100 // wait 100 ms
Waiting:
 gettick nowTick
  brcmp LT, Waiting, nowTick, thenTick  // time up?
jmp Forever

 exit
endt
```

Listing C-2. *voltmeter.nbc*

```
//------------------Variable Declarations------------------
dseg segment

TLocation      struct
 X             sword
 Y             sword
TLocation      ends
TDrawText      struct
 Result        sbyte
 Location      TLocation
 Text          byte[]
 Options       dword
TDrawText      ends
dtArgs TDrawText
```

```
thePort byte IN_1 // sensor port 1
theSensorType byte IN_TYPE_REFLECTION  // RCX style light
theSensorMode byte IN_MODE_RAW  // raw data mode
RVal sword
Scale sword 16  // around 16, determine experimentally
Offset sword 570 // around 570, determine experimentally

SVal sword 0
isInvalid byte
thenTick dword
nowTick dword

dseg ends

//-----------------Program Code--------------------------
thread main

 set dtArgs.Location.X, 40
 set dtArgs.Location.Y, 30
 set dtArgs.Options, 1        // clear screen

 setin  theSensorType, thePort, Type    // write sensor type to port
 setin  theSensorMode, thePort, InputMode // write sensor mode to port
 set    isInvalid, TRUE  // invalidate the sensor
 // sensor reset sequence
 setin  isInvalid, thePort, InvalidData
stillInvalid:   // loop until it is not invalid
 getin  isInvalid, thePort, InvalidData
 brtst  NEQ, stillInvalid, isInvalid
setin   SVal, thePort, ScaledValue // reset the scaled value

Forever:
 getin  RVal, thePort, RawValue  // read in new value
 sub RVal, Offset, RVal // remove offset    RVal = Offset - RVal
 mul RVal, RVal, Scale  // scale to volts   RVal = RVal * Scale
 div RVal, RVal, 10     // adjust to mV     RVal = RVal /10
 numtostr dtArgs.Text, RVal  // convert number to string
 syscall DrawText, dtArgs    // display number
 gettick nowTick  // what time is it now?
 Add    thenTick, nowTick, 100 // wait 100 ms
Waiting:
 gettick nowTick
 brcmp  LT, Waiting, nowTick, thenTick  // time up?
jmp Forever

 exit
endt
```

Listing C-3. *whistler.nbc*

```
#include "NXTdefs.h"
//------------------Variable Declarations------------------
dseg segment
dtArgs TDrawText
PT_A TSoundPlayTone

theIPort byte IN_1 // input port 1
theSensorType byte IN_TYPE_REFLECTION // RCX style light
theSensorMode byte IN_MODE_RAW  // raw mode
SVal sword 0
isInvalid byte

theOPort byte OUT_A   // motor port A
theMode byte OUT_MODE_MOTORON   // mode on
rsVal byte OUT_RUNSTATE_RUNNING  // state running
pwr byte 100  // full power
theUF byte UF_UPDATE_SPEED+UF_UPDATE_MODE  // update flags

RVal sword
Offset sword 400 // around 400, determine experimentally

dseg ends
//-----------------Program Code--------------------------
thread main

  set PT_A.Duration, 50 // .05 sec
  set PT_A.Loop, 0   // no looping
  set PT_A.Volume, 3    // percent/25
  set dtArgs.Location.X, 40  // X location for text
  set dtArgs.Location.Y, 40  // Y location for text
  set dtArgs.Options, 1 // erase screen

  setin  theSensorType, theIPort, Type     // write sensor type to port
  setin  theSensorMode, theIPort, InputMode // write sensor mode to port
  set    isInvalid, TRUE  // invalidate the sensor
  // sensor reset sequence
  setin  isInvalid, theIPort, InvalidData
stillInvalid:   // loop until it is not invalid
  getin  isInvalid, theIPort, InvalidData
  brtst  NEQ, stillInvalid, isInvalid
  setin  SVal, theIPort, ScaledValue // reset the scaled value

   // turn output port A full power
setout theOPort, OutputMode, theMode, RunState, rsVal, Power, pwr,
 UpdateFlags, theUF
```

```
forever:

  getin  RVal, theIPort, RawValue   // read new value
  sub RVal, Offset, RVal  // RVal = Offset - RVal
  numtostr dtArgs.Text, RVal  // convert RVal to string
  syscall DrawText, dtArgs    // display on screen
  mul RVal, RVal, 10  // scale tone up by 10
  mov PT_A.Frequency, RVal   // set tone freq
  syscall SoundPlayTone, PT_A   // play the tone

jmp forever

 exit
endt
```

Listing C-4. *pressuremeter.nbc*

```
//------------------Variable Declarations------------------
dseg segment

TLocation     struct
 X            sword
 Y            sword
TLocation     ends
TDrawText     struct
 Result       sbyte
 Location     TLocation
 Text         byte[]
 Options      dword
TDrawText     ends
dtArgs TDrawText

thePort byte IN_1 // sensor port 1
theSensorType byte IN_TYPE_REFLECTION  // RCX style light
theSensorMode byte IN_MODE_RAW  // raw data mode
RVal sword
Scale sword 6  // approximately 6, but determine experimentally
Offset sword 580 // approximately 580, but determine experimentally

SVal sword 0
isInvalid byte
thenTick dword
nowTick dword

dseg ends
```

```
//-----------------Program Code-------------------------
thread main

 set dtArgs.Location.X, 40
 set dtArgs.Location.Y, 30
 set dtArgs.Options, 1        // clear screen

 setin  theSensorType, thePort, Type     // write sensor type to port
 setin  theSensorMode, thePort, InputMode // write sensor mode to port
 set    isInvalid, TRUE  // invalidate the sensor
 // sensor reset sequence
 setin  isInvalid, thePort, InvalidData
stillInvalid:   // loop until it is not invalid
 getin  isInvalid, thePort, InvalidData
 brtst  NEQ, stillInvalid, isInvalid
setin    SVal, thePort, ScaledValue // reset the scaled value

Forever:
 getin  RVal, thePort, RawValue  // read in new value
 sub RVal, RVal, Offset // remove offset   RVal = RVal - Offset
 div RVal, RVal, Scale  // scale to volts  RVal = RVal / Scale
 numtostr dtArgs.Text, RVal  // convert number to string
 syscall DrawText, dtArgs     // display number
 gettick nowTick  // what time is it now?
 add    thenTick, nowTick, 100 // wait 100 ms
Waiting:
 gettick nowTick
 brcmp LT, Waiting, nowTick, thenTick  // time up?
jmp Forever

 exit
endt
```

Chapter 13

Listing C-5. *MagicWandLEGO.nbc*

```
#include "NXTDefs.h"
#define TouchPort IN_4
#define I2CPort IN_1
#define I2CAddress 0x40

// 0x40 for PCF8574 or 0x70 for PCF8574A
```

```
// -------------- Variable Declarations --------------
dseg  segment
// Arguments for low speed comm syscalls
   lswArgs TCommLSWrite
   lscsArgs TCommLSCheckStatus
// Display patterns
// Each byte represents a column of dots with last byte = 0
// Bit set to 1 means lit LED.
// Least significant bit is at top of column.
// Maximum number of bytes per pattern: 15
   L_ byte[] 0xff, 0x80, 0x80, 0x80, 0x80, 0x80, 0x80, 0x80, 0
   E_ byte[] 0xff, 0x89, 0x89, 0x89, 0x89, 0x81, 0x81, 0x81, 0
   O_ byte[] 0x7e, 0x81, 0x81, 0x81, 0x81, 0x81, 0x81, 0x7e, 0
   G_ byte[] 0x7e, 0x81, 0x81, 0x81, 0x81, 0x91, 0x90, 0x72, 0
// Misc
   DispBuf byte[]
   sVal byte
dseg ends
// ---------------- Program Code ----------------
thread main
// Init variables
   set lswArgs.ReturnLen, 0 // only send data
   mov lswArgs.Port, I2CPort
// Init Touch Sensor, used to detect leftmost position of sweep
   SetSensorType(TouchPort,IN_TYPE_SWITCH)
   SetSensorMode(TouchPort,IN_MODE_BOOLEAN)
   ResetSensor(TouchPort)
// Initialize input port to I2C
   SetSensorType(I2CPort,IN_TYPE_LOWSPEED)
   SetSensorMode(I2CPort,IN_MODE_RAW)
   ResetSensor(I2CPort)
// Start Motor, full speed
   OnFwd(OUT_A, 100)
Forever:
// --------- Display LEGO message -----------------
   call WaitTouch // Wait for start
   wait 20  // Wait a little to center display
   mov DispBuf, L_
   call DispLetter
   mov DispBuf, E_
   call DispLetter
   mov DispBuf, G_
   call DispLetter
   mov DispBuf, O_
   call DispLetter
   jmp Forever  // Start over
endt
```

```
// Wait for end of sweep touch pressed, then released
subroutine WaitTouch
TouchLoopP:  // Wait for touch sensor pressed
   getin sVal, TouchPort, ScaledValue
   brtst EQ, TouchLoopP, sVal
TouchLoopR:  // then released
   getin sVal, TouchPort, ScaledValue
   brtst NEQ, TouchLoopR, sVal
   return
ends


// Sends the buffer containing the pattern to be displayed. Each column
// is displayed during the time needed to send a byte, about 1ms
subroutine DispLetter
   xor DispBuf, DispBuf, 0xff // Invert all bytes of display buffer
   arrbuild lswArgs.Buffer, I2CAddress, DispBuf // Prepare buffer
StatWait:  // Wait for the end of previously sent data
   syscall CommLSCheckStatus, lscsArgs
   brtst GT, StatWait, lscsArgs.Result
   syscall CommLSWrite, lswArgs  // Send new buffer
   return
ends
```

Listing C-6. *simon.nbc*

```
#include "NXTDefs.h"
// -------------- Variable Declarations --------------
#define I2CPort IN_1
#define I2CAddress 0x40
// 0x40 for PCF8574 or 0x70 for PCF8574A
#define MaxNotes 50
#define ToneDuration 300
#define IntervalDuration 100


dseg    segment
  lswArgs TCommLSWrite        // Write structure
  lscsArgs TCommLSCheckStatus // Status structure
  lsrArgs TCommLSRead         // Read structure
  btnArgs TReadButton         // NXT button read

  notes byte[]
  ToneFreq word[] {TONE_C4, TONE_E4, TONE_G4, TONE_C5}

  i word
  j word
  button word
  Value byte
  Prev byte
```

```
    LTarg byte
    GBval byte
    Tone word


dseg ends
// --------------- Program Code ----------------
thread main
// Initialize variables
    mov lswArgs.Port, I2CPort
    mov lsrArgs.Port, I2CPort
    mov lscsArgs.Port, I2CPort
    set lsrArgs.BufferLen, 1  // Read 1 byte
// Initialize input port to I2C
    SetSensorType(I2CPort,IN_TYPE_LOWSPEED)
    SetSensorMode(I2CPort,IN_MODE_RAW)
    ResetSensor(I2CPort)
    TextOut(8, 48, 1, 'NXT Simon')
    TextOut(8, 32, 0, 'Press orange')
    TextOut(8, 24, 0, 'button to start')

StartLoop:
    Random(Value,4)
// Wait for button and seed random
    set btnArgs.Index, 3
    syscall ReadButton, btnArgs
    brtst EQ, StartLoop, btnArgs.Pressed
    TextOut(8, 32, 0, '            ')
    TextOut(8, 24, 0, '               ')
// Init notes array, without repetition
    arrinit notes, 0, MaxNotes
    replace notes, notes, 0, Value
    mov Prev, Value
    set i, 1
NoteInit:
    Random(Value,4)
    brcmp EQ, NoteInit, Value, Prev
    replace notes, notes, i, Value
    mov Prev, Value
    add i, i, 1
    brcmp NEQ, NoteInit, i, MaxNotes
    set i, 1
MainLoop:
    set j,0
PlayTune:
    index LTarg, notes, j
    call LedTone
    add j,j,1
    brcmp NEQ, PlayTune, j,i
```

```
    set j,0
CheckTune:
    call GetButtons
    index Value, notes, j
    brcmp NEQ, GameOver, Value, GBval
    mov LTarg, Value
    call LedTone
    add j,j,1
    brcmp NEQ, CheckTune, j,i

    wait 1000
    add i, i, 1
    brcmp NEQ, MainLoop, i, MaxNotes
GameOver:
    TextOut(10, 48, 1, 'Game Over!')
    TextOut(10, 32, 0, 'Level Reached')
    NumOut(10, 24, 0, i)

    PlayTone(TONE_C6, 100)
    wait 100
    PlayTone(TONE_G5, 120)
    wait 120
    PlayTone(TONE_E5, 150)
    wait 150
    PlayTone(TONE_C5, 170)
    wait 170
    PlayTone(TONE_G4, 200)
    wait 5000
endt


//*****************************************
// Plays a tone and light matching LED.
// LEDs are on the upper half of sent byte
// Value passed in LTarg

subroutine LedTone

dseg segment
    Led byte
    LTi byte
dseg ends

    set Led, 0x10
    mov LTi, LTarg
LTLoop:
    brtst EQ, SendPattern, LTi
    mul Led, Led, 2
```

```
    sub LTi, LTi, 1
    jmp LTLoop
SendPattern:
    xor Led, Led, 0xff
    arrbuild lswArgs.Buffer, I2CAddress, Led
    set lswArgs.ReturnLen, 0 // Read 0 byte
    syscall CommLSWrite, lswArgs
LTWait: // Wait til done
    syscall CommLSCheckStatus, lscsArgs
    brtst GT, LTWait, lscsArgs.Result

// play tone
    index Tone, ToneFreq, LTarg
    PlayTone(Tone,ToneDuration)
    wait ToneDuration
// Leds off
    arrbuild lswArgs.Buffer, I2CAddress, 0xff
    set lswArgs.ReturnLen, 0 // Read 0 byte
    syscall CommLSWrite, lswArgs
LTWait2: // Wait til done
    syscall CommLSCheckStatus, lscsArgs
    brtst GT, LTWait2, lscsArgs.Result
    return
ends


//*******************************************
// Reads the I2C button state and returns button number
// The buttons are on lower half of read byte
// Value returned in GBval

subroutine GetButtons

BtnLoop:
    arrbuild lswArgs.Buffer, I2CAddress, 0xff
    set lswArgs.ReturnLen, 1 // Read 1 byte
    syscall CommLSWrite, lswArgs
BtnWait: // Wait til done
    syscall CommLSCheckStatus, lscsArgs
    brtst GT, BtnWait, lscsArgs.Result
    syscall CommLSRead, lsrArgs
    index Value, lsrArgs.Buffer, 0
    xor Value, Value, 0xff
    brtst EQ, BtnLoop, Value
    set GBval, 0
BtnDecode:
    div Value, Value, 2
    brtst EQ, BtnFound, Value
```

```
    add GBval, GBval, 1
    jmp BtnDecode
BtnFound:
    return
ends
```

Listing C-7. *colorsensor_CdS.nbc*

```
#include "NXTDefs.h"
#define I2CPort IN_1
#define TouchPort IN_2
#define I2CAddress 0x40

dseg    segment

Color struct
  Red word
  Green word
  Blue word
ends

    lswArgs TCommLSWrite        // Write structure
    lscsArgs TCommLSCheckStatus // Status structure

    RawColor Color
    ScaledColor Color

    Hue sword
    Led byte
    Light word

    Value byte

    MaxIntens word
    MinIntens word
    DiffIntens word

dseg ends
// ---------------- Program Code ----------------
thread main
// Initialize variables
    mov lswArgs.Port, I2CPort
    mov lscsArgs.Port, I2CPort
    set lswArgs.ReturnLen, 0

// Initialize input port to I2C
    SetSensorType(I2CPort,IN_TYPE_LOWSPEED)
```

```
    SetSensorMode(I2CPort,IN_MODE_RAW)
    ResetSensor(I2CPort)

// Init port 2 as touch sensor
    SetSensorTouch(TouchPort)
    ResetSensor(TouchPort)

//----------------Top of loop---------------
Loop:  // Top of loop

    call ReadHue

    TextOut(6, 48, 1, 'Red')
    NumOut(42, 48, 0, RawColor.Red)
    TextOut(6, 40, 0, 'Green')
    NumOut(42, 40, 0, RawColor.Green)
    TextOut(6, 32, 0, 'Blue')
    NumOut(42, 32, 0, RawColor.Blue)

    TextOut(6, 16, 0, 'Hue')
    NumOut(42, 16, 0, Hue)

// Wait for touch sensor press and release

WaitPress:
    ReadSensor(TouchPort, Value)
    brtst EQ, WaitPress, Value
WaitRelease:
    ReadSensor(TouchPort, Value)
    brtst NEQ, WaitRelease, Value
// Start over
    jmp Loop
endt


// input Led (1,4,0x10) -> led to light
// output Light -> reflected light level
subroutine ReadColorComponent
    xor Value, Led, 0xff
    arrbuild lswArgs.Buffer, I2CAddress, Value
    syscall CommLSWrite, lswArgs
Wait1: // Wait til done
    syscall CommLSCheckStatus, lscsArgs
    brtst GT, Wait1, lscsArgs.Result
    wait 20
    ReadSensor(I2CPort,Light)
    sub Light, 1024, Light
    arrbuild lswArgs.Buffer, I2CAddress, 0xff
    syscall CommLSWrite, lswArgs
```

```
Wait2: // Wait til done
   syscall CommLSCheckStatus, lscsArgs
   brtst GT, Wait2, lscsArgs.Result
   wait 10
   return
ends


// ReadHue returns calculated color hue in Hue

subroutine ReadHue
   set Led, 1
   call ReadColorComponent
   mul RawColor.Blue, Light, 10
   set Led, 4
   call ReadColorComponent
   mul RawColor.Red, Light, 10
   set Led, 0x10
   call ReadColorComponent
   mul RawColor.Green, Light, 10


//   MaxIntens = max( max(Blue, Red), Green)
//   MinIntens = min( min(Blue, Red), Green)
//   DiffIntens = (MaxIntens - MinIntens)/60
   #pragma debugbreak
   mov MaxIntens, RawColor.Red
   brcmp GT, RH1, MaxIntens, RawColor.Green
   mov MaxIntens, RawColor.Green
RH1:
   brcmp GT, RH2, MaxIntens, RawColor.Blue
   mov MaxIntens, RawColor.Blue
RH2:
   mov MinIntens, RawColor.Red
   brcmp LT, RH3, MinIntens, RawColor.Green
   mov MinIntens, RawColor.Green
RH3:
   brcmp LT, RH4, MinIntens, RawColor.Blue
   mov MinIntens, RawColor.Blue
RH4:
   sub DiffIntens, MaxIntens, MinIntens
   div DiffIntens, DiffIntens, 60

   sub ScaledColor.Red, MaxIntens, RawColor.Red
   div ScaledColor.Red, ScaledColor.Red, DiffIntens
   sub ScaledColor.Green, MaxIntens, RawColor.Green
   div ScaledColor.Green, ScaledColor.Green, DiffIntens
   sub ScaledColor.Blue, MaxIntens, RawColor.Blue
   div ScaledColor.Blue, ScaledColor.Blue, DiffIntens
```

```
   brcmp NEQ, RH5, MaxIntens, RawColor.Blue
   add Hue, 240, ScaledColor.Green
   sub Hue, Hue, ScaledColor.Red
RH5:
   brcmp NEQ, RH6, MaxIntens, RawColor.Green
   add Hue, 120, ScaledColor.Red
   sub Hue, Hue, ScaledColor.Blue
RH6:
   brcmp NEQ, RH7, MaxIntens, RawColor.Red
   sub Hue, ScaledColor.Blue, ScaledColor.Green
RH7:
   brtst GT, RH8, Hue
   add Hue, Hue, 360
RH8:
   return
ends
```

Listing C-8. *atod.nbc*

```
#include "NXTDefs.h"
// -------------- Variable Declarations --------------
#define I2CPort IN_1
#define I2CAddress 0x90
dseg    segment
Tatod   struct
   ch0 byte
   ch1 byte
   ch2 byte
   ch3 byte
Tatod ends
   atod Tatod                 // AtoD structure
   lswArgs TCommLSWrite       // Write structure
   lscsArgs TCommLSCheckStatus // Status structure
   lsrArgs TCommLSRead        // Read structure
   count word
dseg ends
// ---------------- Program Code ----------------
thread main
   // Initialize variables
   mov lswArgs.Port, I2CPort
   mov lsrArgs.Port, I2CPort
   mov lscsArgs.Port, I2CPort
   arrbuild lswArgs.Buffer, I2CAddress, 0x04 // auto increment
   set lswArgs.ReturnLen, 5
   set lsrArgs.BufferLen, 5
Top: // Initialize input port to I2C
   SetSensorType(I2CPort,IN_TYPE_LOWSPEED)
```

```
    SetSensorMode(I2CPort,IN_MODE_RAW)
    ResetSensor(I2CPort)
Loop: // Main Loop
    call Atod4    // Get new values
    NumOut(1,60,1,count)
    TextOut(1,38,0,'Ch0')
    NumOut(28,38,0,atod.ch0)
    TextOut(1,30,0,'Ch1')
    NumOut(28,30,0,atod.ch1)
    TextOut(1,22,0,'Ch2')
    NumOut(28,22,0,atod.ch2)
    TextOut(1,14,0,'Ch3')
    NumOut(28,14,0,atod.ch3)
    add count, count, 1
    // Start over
    jmp Loop
endt

subroutine Atod4
Atod4top:
    syscall CommLSWrite, lswArgs
Atod4Wait:
    syscall CommLSCheckStatus, lscsArgs
    brtst GT, Atod4Wait, lscsArgs.Result
    brcmp NEQ, Atod4top, lscsArgs.BytesReady, 5
    syscall CommLSRead, lsrArgs
    index atod.ch0, lsrArgs.Buffer, 1
    index atod.ch1, lsrArgs.Buffer, 2
    index atod.ch2, lsrArgs.Buffer, 3
    index atod.ch3, lsrArgs.Buffer, 4
    return
ends
```

Chapter 14

Listing C-9. *pong.nbc*

```
#include "NXTDefs.h"
// -------------- Variable Declarations --------------
#define I2CPort IN_1
#define I2CAddress 0x90

dseg segment
// a to d channels
    Ch2 byte
    Ch3 byte
```

```
// syscall structures
   lswArgs TCommLSWrite
   lscsArgs TCommLSCheckStatus
   lsrArgs TCommLSRead
// Graphic structures
   ball TDrawGraphic
   lpad TDrawGraphic
   rpad TDrawGraphic
// Various Variables
   z sword
   x byte 6
   y byte 30
   xvel byte 1
   yvel byte 1
   rpady byte
   lpady byte
   rscore byte 0
   lscore byte 0
dseg ends
// --------------- Program Code ----------------
thread main
// Initialize variables
   set ball.Options, 0
   set lpad.Options, 0
   set lpad.Location.Y, 0
   set lpad.Location.X, 5
   set rpad.Options, 0
   set rpad.Location.Y, 0
   set rpad.Location.X, 95
   NumOut(78,60,0,rscore)
   NumOut(20,60,0,lscore)
// Initialize I2C
   mov lswArgs.Port, I2CPort
   mov lsrArgs.Port, I2CPort
   mov lscsArgs.Port, I2CPort
   arrbuild lswArgs.Buffer, I2CAddress, 0x04 // auto incr
   set lswArgs.ReturnLen, 5
   set lsrArgs.BufferLen, 5
   SetSensorType(I2CPort,IN_TYPE_LOWSPEED)
   SetSensorMode(I2CPort,IN_MODE_RAW)
   ResetSensor(I2CPort)
top:
   NumOut(78,60,0,rscore)
   NumOut(20,60,0,lscore)
   call Atod4    // Get new values
   div lpady, Ch3, 4    // Pot on CH3 and scale
   mov lpad.Filename, 'N.RIC'  // erase left pad
```

```
     syscall DrawGraphic lpad
     mov lpad.Location.Y, lpady   // draw left pad
     mov lpad.Filename, 'P.RIC'
     syscall DrawGraphic lpad
     div rpady, Ch2, 4    // Pot on CH2 and scale
     mov rpad.Filename, 'N.RIC'  // erase right pad
     syscall DrawGraphic rpad
     mov rpad.Location.Y, rpady  // draw right pad
     mov rpad.Filename, 'P.RIC'
     syscall DrawGraphic rpad
     mov ball.Filename, 'W.RIC'  // erase ball
     syscall DrawGraphic ball
     add x, x, xvel              // move ball
     add y, y, yvel
     mov ball.Location.X, x      // draw ball
     mov ball.Location.Y, y
     mov ball.Filename, 'B.RIC'
     syscall DrawGraphic ball
chk0:  // off left side?
     brcmp LT, chk1, x, 96
     set x, 6
     set y, 30
     add lscore, lscore, 1
     jmp razz
chk1:  // off right side?
     brcmp GT, chk2, x, 2
     set x, 94
     set y, 30
     add rscore, rscore, 1
razz:  // noise and score
     PlayTone(100, 500)
     wait 500
     jmp top
chk2:  // bounce off top?
     brcmp LT, chk3, y, 60
     set yvel, -1
chk3:  // bounce off bottom?
     brcmp GT, chk4, y, 1
     set yvel, 1
chk4:  // bounce off left paddle?
     brcmp NEQ, chk5, x, 5
     add z, lpady, 6
     sub z, z, y
     abs z, z
     brcmp GT, chk5, z, 10
     set xvel, 1
     PlayTone(600, 50)
```

```
chk5:   // bounce off right paddle?
    brcmp NEQ, chk6, x, 93
    add z, rpady, 6
    sub z, z, y
    abs z, z
    brcmp GT, chk6, z, 10
    set xvel, -1
    PlayTone(600, 50)
chk6:
    wait 15  // 10 fast - 30 slow
    jmp top
endt

subroutine Atod4
Atod4top:
    syscall CommLSWrite, lswArgs
Atod4Wait:
    syscall CommLSCheckStatus, lscsArgs
    brtst GT, Atod4Wait, lscsArgs.Result
    brcmp NEQ, Atod4top, lscsArgs.BytesReady, 5
    syscall CommLSRead, lsrArgs
    index Ch2, lsrArgs.Buffer, 3
    index Ch3, lsrArgs.Buffer, 4
    return
ends
```

Index

forums.apress.com

FOR PROFESSIONALS BY PROFESSIONALS™

JOIN THE APRESS FORUMS AND BE PART OF OUR COMMUNITY. You'll find discussions that cover topics of interest to IT professionals, programmers, and enthusiasts just like you. If you post a query to one of our forums, you can expect that some of the best minds in the business—especially Apress authors, who all write with *The Expert's Voice*™—will chime in to help you. Why not aim to become one of our most valuable participants (MVPs) and win cool stuff? Here's a sampling of what you'll find:

DATABASES

Data drives everything.

Share information, exchange ideas, and discuss any database programming or administration issues.

INTERNET TECHNOLOGIES AND NETWORKING

Try living without plumbing (and eventually IPv6).

Talk about networking topics including protocols, design, administration, wireless, wired, storage, backup, certifications, trends, and new technologies.

JAVA

We've come a long way from the old Oak tree.

Hang out and discuss Java in whatever flavor you choose: J2SE, J2EE, J2ME, Jakarta, and so on.

MAC OS X

All about the Zen of OS X.

OS X is both the present and the future for Mac apps. Make suggestions, offer up ideas, or boast about your new hardware.

OPEN SOURCE

Source code is good; understanding (open) source is better.

Discuss open source technologies and related topics such as PHP, MySQL, Linux, Perl, Apache, Python, and more.

PROGRAMMING/BUSINESS

Unfortunately, it is.

Talk about the Apress line of books that cover software methodology, best practices, and how programmers interact with the "suits."

WEB DEVELOPMENT/DESIGN

Ugly doesn't cut it anymore, and CGI is absurd.

Help is in sight for your site. Find design solutions for your projects and get ideas for building an interactive Web site.

SECURITY

Lots of bad guys out there—the good guys need help.

Discuss computer and network security issues here. Just don't let anyone else know the answers!

TECHNOLOGY IN ACTION

Cool things. Fun things.

It's after hours. It's time to play. Whether you're into LEGO® MINDSTORMS™ or turning an old PC into a DVR, this is where technology turns into fun.

WINDOWS

No defenestration here.

Ask questions about all aspects of Windows programming, get help on Microsoft technologies covered in Apress books, or provide feedback on any Apress Windows book.

HOW TO PARTICIPATE:

Go to the Apress Forums site at **http://forums.apress.com/**.

Click the New User link.

You Need the Companion eBook